for sinners only

*If God lived on earth
people would break His windows.*

for sinners only

Perspectives on the Lord's Supper
drawn from the life of St. Paul

by

J. D. EPPINGA

WILLIAM B. EERDMANS / PUBLISHER
GRAND RAPIDS, MICHIGAN

To the members of the
LaGrave Avenue Christian Reformed Church
who gave me time to write this book.

CONTENTS

1

THE THRESHOLD OF THE UPPER ROOM

The church of my childhood observed the holy sacrament of communion four times a year. These four services were always very special and, I might add, very long. Whenever I entered the sanctuary on a Sunday morning and saw that the table had been moved to front and center and covered with a pure white linen cloth, I knew I would have to sit for about five million hours. After the usual service, including a full-length sermon, the minister would begin reading the Lord's Supper formulary, itself a seemingly endless affair, after which there would follow extra songs, an extra offering, and the distribution of the elements.

Immediately before the celebration proper, there was always a terrible congestion in the aisles as communicants moved forward and non-communicants retired to the rear of the church.

I was a noncommunicant. Not being considered old enough, I too had to move to the back, where I found myself a place, feeling rather lonely and abandoned by my parents. Sitting very still, having been forewarned not to move a muscle, I observed the proceedings from this vantage point with a feeling of awe and respect. It was the sort of situation in which, if you itched anywhere, you didn't scratch. On the closing hymn I always exhaled on the first line of the first verse, as if I had been holding my breath for a very long time, which, in a certain sense, was true.

This is not meant to be disrespectful. True, the experience was not without its limitations. A child psychologist could find things to criticize. In retrospect, however, I find that I did some of my most serious thinking on precisely these occasions. What does the wine taste like? Is the bread just ordinary bread? Will I ever be good enough to participate myself? Probably not, I thought. Surely not as long as I laughed at a dirty story, as I had the day before. But then, what about Mr. A., who was participating even though it had been whispered by some that he had gone to a picture show! Was he, in fact, eating and drinking judgment unto himself?

The older I became, the more I pondered at communion time, particularly this matter of eating and drinking personal judgment or damnation, a phrase repeated in the formulary and taken from 1 Corinthians 11:29. Why not be wholly safe and abstain forever, instead of running such a risk? Counterbalancing this inclination, however, was the Lord's command, "This do" (Luke 22:19). He had said it in the language of the imperative. But perhaps this was addressed only to saints like Mr. B, a perennial elder, aged and devout and, very probably, without sin, or nearly so.

On my first communion, moving uncertainly forward instead of to the rear as had been my custom, I was conscious of the eyes of some of my peers who still occupied observers' benches. Was my action saying to them that I now felt myself to be better? Holier? Superior? Even so, my first participation was a good experience, which found me more sensitive to the meaning of the sacrament than many later occasions when I had grown more accustomed to it all. Still, the questions persisted. Did I really belong at the table of the Lord? Was it a place for frauds like me?

Today I stand on the other side of the table as a minister of the gospel. It is a privilege undeserved. When officiating, during those moments of silence when the elements are being distributed, I wonder sometimes what each is thinking. Perhaps the children's thoughts approximate mine of years ago. Some people may be partaking for the first time. For them the hour will no doubt hold a special sacredness. Others may be withholding themselves on the grounds that they are not yet ready or good enough or do not yet know enough.

I remember that years ago I discussed some of these matters with my pastor, a wise and understanding man. He had much good advice to give.

Confessing Christ, he said, was as much an act of the will as an impulse of the heart. It was a positive response to the Master's voice calling to us to follow Him. "In attempting this, you stumble and fall a lot," the minister added, "but each time you pick yourself up again, and in the fellowship of other Christians you continue in His direction." Being encouraged by words like these to make my commitment did not, however, ease my mind on the question of communion.

"The Bible says," I said (not knowing precisely where), "that you must examine yourself before participation. It is exactly such inventory, however, that discourages attendance at the table."

In response, my pastor cited the fact that though self-analysis was required, it was not to determine worthiness, which all of us utterly lack, but motive, which must be right, and repentance, which must be sincere. This helped somewhat, even though I had not been entirely ignorant of these refinements and distinctions. It was what he added that made the visit memorable. Turning to a Bible on the table between us, he said something I have since learned to say to others. "You quoted Scripture a moment ago, which is always a dangerous thing to do unless you find and read your reference precisely and exactly." Confessing that I was not able to locate my quotation, he turned the pages to 1 Corinthians 11:28 and read, "Let a man examine himself, and so eat of the bread and drink of the cup."

"Precisely," I said (though in teen-age language), "and that's the problem. It would be simpler to come to communion if this were not required, and almost impossible because it is."

"Well, let us see," continued my mentor, "who is saying this? It is Paul, a man with a closet chock full of skeletons. I am sure that if he urged self-examination on us, he must have engaged in the same spiritual exercise himself. For Paul, unlike the Pharisees (Matthew 23:3), always tried to practice what he preached. Now, Christian introspection must have made him heartsore. It led him, in fact, to label himself the chief of sinners (1 Timothy 1:15). So, if he could look back on his sad record and still come to the table of communion, then, perhaps, you can as well. Surely, you must agree that Paul's diary had pages in it that were, to put it mildly, as bad as anyone's."

It was a new angle. I was quite familiar, of course, with the life of Paul, having heard about it a hundred times at home, in church, and at the Christian School. He had never appealed to me, to tell the truth. He had always come through, in my mind, as someone imperious, intellectual, and cold. I liked Peter much better, and John most of all. But now, dimly, Paul began to emerge in my eyes as a human figure of flesh and blood.

Since that time, Paul has grown on me. It really must have been hard for him when he reviewed himself, as it were, in preparation for communion. I have frequently tried to imagine his thoughts on such occasions, and this has helped me in my personal preparation for communion.

13

I propose, therefore, that in the following pages we examine together the life of one who told us to examine our own lives each time we celebrate the sacrament. Perhaps those who hesitate will be emboldened, while others, coming for their first communion, will be instructed. Perhaps, too, those for whom undue familiarity with the table has produced a measure of spiritual insensitivity may find a new and more meaningful approach.

To be forewarned, our study will be more devotional than scholarly; more practical than biographical; or, if you like big words, more homiletical than exegetical. So, come along. If the following pages do you no good at all, the fault will be mine — not Paul's.

*　*　*　*　*

Ideally, you should read what follows with your Bible within reach. If you are like me, however, you may not take the time to look up each of the textual references. Accordingly, they are quoted in full in the back of the book, either from the King James Version or the Revised Standard Version. This makes it as easy as possible for you to consult the biblical references and will, hopefully, enrich your perusal of these pages.

2

THE PLUME OF PEDIGREE

Matthew, Mark, Luke, and John all begin
the story of Jesus Christ in different ways. Like-
wise, there are various approaches we could take
to the life of the man who wrote the biggest part
of the New Testament and who ever stands as
the church's greatest missionary. We shall initi-
ate ourselves into the life of Paul by way of a
slow and careful reading of his words in Philippians 3, beginning at verse three. Consider them
reflectively: ". . . and put no confidence in the
flesh. Though I myself have reason for confidence
in the flesh also. If any other man thinks he has
reason for confidence in the flesh, I have more:
circumcised on the eighth day, of the people of
Israel, of the tribe of Benjamin, a Hebrew born
of Hebrews. . . ."

I am sure that you understand what is meant
by the word "pedigree." It is something that has
to do with your genealogy, with your lineage,
with your line of descent. Generally speaking,
whatever that line of descent may be, you are

proud of it. Furthermore, you may say, "not only was I born there, but my father, and his father, and his father before him; and so, not only am I a fourth-generation American, but a fourth-generation Californian, of which there are not many." Perhaps you proudly trace your ancestors to a certain country in Europe or Africa or Asia and, more than that, to a certain province of that country. As often as you cite this fact, and in a lifetime you cite it more often than you realize, you wear it as a feather in your cap. A plume. It is the plume of pedigree.

You meet a certain gentleman, let us say, who seems condescending towards you — a thing to which you take understandable exception. And so you say to another, "You'd think, from the way he talks, that his ancestors came over on the Mayflower." Maybe they did; maybe they did not. If you discover that they did, you will probably say "So what?" out of sheer jealousy. But if, on the other hand, yours did, you will, no doubt, publish the fact in boldest print. "My ancestors hail from Boston!" That's a feather. "I'm a Texan!" Another feather. Or, "I'm a Van Updike from New Amsterdam." Or, again, "I'm an F.F.V." (First Families of Virginia). In many subtle ways, we take the feathers away from the Indians for our own proud headdress.

The late and unlamented Adolf Hitler made much of pedigree. You had to be Aryan, a pure-blood of good stock. If you had even a little bit of Jewish blood in your veins, you had to hide that fact for your life. But in the synagogue then, as now, the rabbi said to the boy, "Son, you are Jewish. Be proud of that." Meanwhile, on this little planet dwarfed in space some little creatures with little pigmentation in their skins become "white" supremacists, while others of a darker hue, standing equally on tiptoe, shout that black is beautiful. Don't ever make the mistake of calling a Ukrainian a Russian. He will correct you, and severely too. Remember the caste of an Indian, and the Australian who is natively an Australian, and do not arouse the ire of an Irishman by mistaking him for an Englishman or a Scot, or the other way around. Don't forget that so-and-so is high born, and that his grandfather was Colonel So-and-so, who fought in the Battle of What's-its-name.

In all of this, we see a picture of ourselves and of all men everywhere.

I have a dog at home — a pedigreed dog. The fact that I tell you she is pedigreed already betrays a trait in me. Some time ago our dog's sire had his picture in the paper, having won a national championship over stiff competition. Just for fun, we showed the picture to our dog, laughed, and observed that it was a good thing our Pal was illiterate. For, could she have read the article, she would proably have pulled up her nose at all of us. But dogs don't do such things — even the highly pedigreed. Only people do.

Paul was a prime example. He had a lineage as long as your arm, and a Class A pedigree. That is what he writes about in his letter to the Philippians.

He tells them that he was circumcised the eighth day. In other words, he was "of the circumcision," a fact that placed him among the elite of the earth. But what is most significant is the fact that he was circumcised the eighth day — a truly tremendous distinction. If you were an Ishmaelite, for example, Jewish law said you could not have this rite performed until you were thirteen years of age. If you were a convert to the Jewish faith, a proselyte, you were circumcised upon entry into the synagogue, in youth, the middle years, or later. It was a great privilege to receive this rite at whatever age, but it was an even higher privilege to be born of parents, both of whom were of the proper stand religiously. So it was with Jesus. It was therefore possible for Him to be circumcised the eighth day, as Luke tells us in the Christmas story (Luke 2:21). So, too, with Paul. "Circumcised the eighth day" meant that he was born of proper parents. "Circumcised the eighth day" meant that both his father and his mother were fully conformed to all the strict requirements of Jewish law. Thus, Paul meant to say, he was a true blueblood from birth.

But not only did he point out that he was circumcised the eighth day. He added to this another plume: to wit, "of the people of Israel." The King James Version says "of the stock of Israel."

You've heard, if not used, the expression many times. "Of good stock," we say. Paul meant to imply by this that his parents were not proselytes, nor theirs, and so on, but Israelites all the way. Some people could only claim Abraham for their father — not Isaac. And some people could only claim Abraham and Isaac as their ancestors — not Jacob — for both of these men had children by other wives. But Paul was of the stock of Israel. He came from Abraham and Isaac and Jacob, who was given the covenant name of Israel, meaning the elect race (Genesis 32:28), and Paul was proud to claim his membership therein.

Listen again as Paul boasts of yet another feather in his cap. Not only was he circumcised the eighth day, not only was he of the stock of Israel, but he was of the tribe of Benjamin. Said Paul by implication, "I come from the tribe that gave Israel its first king (1 Samuel 9:1,2). I come from the only tribe that did not swerve in its allegiance to the house of Judah and of David (1 Kings 12:21). I come from the tribe that united with Judah and the Levites after the captivity to rebuild the temple (Ezra 1:5). I come from the tribe within whose boundaries the holy city of Jerusalem stood (Joshua 18:21a,28a). I come from the tribe out of which came Queen Esther and noble Mordecai" (Esther 2:5). Of all the histories of the twelve tribes, that of Benjamin was among the more illustrious.

One might think that there were no more plumes that Paul could preen. How could he add anything more? How could he top what, so far, he had listed as credentials? Yet he did. Not only was he circumcised the eighth day, and of the stock of Israel, and of the tribe of Benjamin, but

(listen to him now) "a Hebrew born of Hebrews."
To understand this tallest and fanciest of all
plumes requires a bit of explanation. All the
children of Israel were called Israelites, but not
all of them were called Hebrews. Only those who
retained the Hebrew language and the Hebrew
customs merited this name. Paul had a father
and a mother who, though living in Tarsus in
Asia Minor, a foreign country with a foreign
culture, nevertheless held on to the Hebrew
language and the Hebrew ways. This was real
faithfulness.

You may know something of how this is. There
are those who emigrate from Europe to America
but who attempt to remain European in language and custom. Others, however, hurriedly
Americanize. So it was two thousand years ago.
There were some Jews of the dispersion who took
on the color and the ways of their surroundings.
But not the family of Paul. They held to their
traditions. Out there in Tarsus they were not
only Israelites, but Hebrews, still holding to all
the ways and laws and language of ancient Moses.
This was real loyalty. It was not surprising, therefore, that Paul's parents sent their son all the way
to Jerusalem, where he perhaps boarded with a
married sister (see Acts 23:16), in order that he
could be trained at the feet of Gamaliel and still
further deepen his roots in the pure soil of
Hebrew culture. No doubt this was costly. But no
matter. They were the Hebrews of the Hebrews,
the cream of the cream.

So, there it is. Not only the plume, but the

pride of pedigree. We all boast. So did Paul, and for what were considered sound reasons. If any man had his foot in the door of heaven, if any man had a corner on God, if any man had the inside track in the race of life for any prizes angels might bestow, it was this well-born star. Not only was he circumcised the eighth day, and of the stock of Israel, and of the tribe of Benjamin, and a Hebrew among Hebrews, but he was a Roman citizen too (Acts 23:27).

But there are two observations to make whenever we emphasize our qualities—Paul's, or yours, or anyone's. First, the more you make of pedigree, the less you make of Christ.

So it was with Paul. From his exalted position he could only look down on the Saviour. Had the hymn been in existence in his day, Paul never would have sung "Nothing in my hands I bring," for his hands, he thought, were full. He never would have sung "Naked come to Thee for dress," for he considered himself clothed with honor and dignity and an inheritance that made him rich from birth.

What was true of Paul is also true of you. The more you make of pedigree, the less you make of Christ. Remember this the next time you so proudly say that you are American, not Russian; or Protestant, not Roman Catholic; or Calvinist, not Lutheran; or white, not black; or the other way around. The more you stand on tiptoe, the less you make of Christ.

The second observation is the reverse of the first; the less you make of pedigree, the more you make of Christ. This, too, was Paul's experience. When he finally came to admit that he was nothing, then to him Christ became everything. When, to quote from his letter to the Philippians again, he "put no confidence in [his] flesh," he placed all confidence in Christ. Again, what is true of Paul, is true of you. It is only when you see the poverty of pedigree that you can behold the wealth of Jesus.

It is not difficult to see that poverty of pedigree. Consider yours: son of Adam, daughter of Eve. But look at Christ's: Son of God, the only begotten of the Father, conceived of the Holy Spirit.

* * * * *

In preparation for communion, it is good to read Philippians 3:3-11. It will help you put a match to your plume, and divest yourself of your pride.

3

LOSS OF MIND

There was a little trouble in the church at Philippi. Nothing big, it was hardly worth noticing at all. There were some differences among the members, a little discord, a little strife just now and then, and some petty jealousies. Yet all of it was hardly enough to notice. Had you been a visitor there some Sunday morning, you would have been aware of none of these things; and even if you had, you would not have been upset. "Par for the course," you would have said. "No church is perfect."

Your attitude would have been normal. The church of Philippi was a fine one. The troubles that existed were minor, the differences negligible, and not worth mentioning to the pastor or the council. No wonder, then, that Paul's letter to them was full of warm affection and gratitude. It was a love letter, really, and a joy to read, both then and now, for we still have that letter available to us, preserved in the Bible. It would have been understandable if Paul had made no reference in it to the people's minor flaws. Perhaps some would even say that it would have been good psychology.

But Paul knew something about how little foxes can spoil vines. So, in the second chapter of his epistle, he made a gentle and indirect reference to their imperfections as a church. He suggested a solution that would always keep their minor troubles minor, even causing them to disappear. Writing to Lydia, a saleswoman in the dye trade, the Philippian prison warden and his family, and all the other members of that congregation, he said, "Let this mind be in you, which was also in Christ Jesus" (Philippians 2:5, KJV). It was as if he was telling them to have the mind of Christ. And when Paul said something about mind, he knew what he was talking about.

Not only did Paul have a pedigree. Circumcised the eighth day, of the stock of Israel, of the tribe of Benjamin, a Hebrew among Hebrews, and a Roman citizen — did not yet represent the sum total of his endowments. In addition to all of this he had a good mind.

It simply isn't true, you see, that everyone is born equal. Already in the nursery differences are apparent. One child has a stronger body than another. Not all infants are equally bright. Life is not a race in which all the runners begin at the same starting line. Some begin with a handicap, while others are given a head start, by no one less than God Himself.

24

Paul was among those who had been given an advantageous beginning. Not only was he born right religiously; not only was he born right socially; not only was he born right politically; but he was also born right intellectually. He had a brilliant mind. Think about how blessed he was and what potentials were his even before he had taken his first step or uttered his first word. Yet, in a recital of his advantages, we must say that what has so far been recounted is not the whole of it.

For besides the many endowments we have cited was the fact that Paul had been divinely placed in a setting in which his good mind could be challenged to develop and grow. Here again was a blessing not so generally conferred at that period of history. Nowadays, more have the opportunity for higher education than formerly. Not too long ago, as our senior citizens can testify, this option was less available. Not all had the chance to finish elementary school, to say nothing of the higher levels. I wonder how many excellent minds have been lost throughout history for the benefit of humanity, because they lacked training and education.

Paul, however, had a father who saw to it that his son learned a trade. In his opinion, apparently, tentmaking was a good one. Probably he reasoned that no matter what happened, Paul would always be able to make a living. But the father wasn't satisfied with that. Paul's mind had to be educated too. And so the son had the privilege and the advantage of schooling. Meanwhile, the home atmosphere was conducive to learning as well, for it was a house with books. Paul's father was a Pharisee. Paul learned Hebrew. Not every boy of the dispersion learned Hebrew, as was intimated in the previous chapter. That is why on Pentecost, when Jews from many places were in Jerusalem, the people heard many languages spoken by those men. But Paul learned Hebrew and Aramaic in the house and Greek on the street. Already as a child, he was multilingual.

Not only did Paul know three languages, but also three cultures — the Hebrew, the Greek, and the Roman. All of this went into the making of his mind. Thoroughly familiar with the Old Testament, he also knew something about Greek thought, Roman law, Stoicism, and paganism (or, as the historians say — the mystery religions). All of it sank into his fertile, able brain.

Like most of us, Paul knew a disadvantage or two. Apparently, he did not have the strongest body. He had an ailment he referred to as "a thorn in the flesh" (2 Corinthians 12:7), so he could not very well enter into any kind of sports program in the local school. He was sorry about this, for he had a great interest in athletics. He knew the best players of his day, as you know them in yours. In later years he referred to the games and the races in his preaching (2 Timothy 4:7). However, even this handicap served to the greater development of the mind of Paul.

When Paul was of a certain age, it was decided that he ought to study under the greatest teacher of them all, the great Gamaliel, himself the student and grandson of the great Hillel. Paul's credentials were sent to Jerusalem. A transcript of his credits was mailed, along with an application to study under the great teacher. And Paul was accepted. He was considered qualified.

All this, too, went into the making of the mind of Paul.

One more fact requires mention: Paul lived in great times (Hebrews 1:1,2a; Galatians 4:4). Some periods in history challenge the minds of men more than others. Some centuries sharpen wits, others leave them dull. Paul lived in a place that quickened brains, in a day when Hebrew, Greek, and Roman lines all crossed. As Dickens said of a later age, "it was the best of times and it was the worst of times," in which a sect called "Nazarenes" and later "Christians" rose to inject a new idea. History's theological and philosophical and political pots were boiling. These were not the dark ages and certainly not the dull ages. On the contrary, if you had a mind, it was a great and stimulating time to be alive. So this, too — the times — went into the making of the mind of Paul.

But enough. Let a man read the Book of Romans — that alone — and thereby be convinced that Paul was one of the mental giants in all of man's story on earth. When God selected the man who would be the church's first missionary, the author of half the New Testament, the great expositor and defender of first-century faith, he went outside the circle of the original twelve, all the way to Tarsus, to choose one of the finest

27

brains He had made and honed. God could and did use an uneducated fisherman like Peter. But for the philosophers in Athens and the lawyers in Rome, he chose a Paul.

We were saying earlier in this chapter that there was a minor problem in the church at Philippi. Some slight discord and strife. It was nothing big, really, just some petty jealousy, pride, and personal vanity. Paul speaks of these things in Philippians 2:3-4. What was to be done about all of this? Paul said there was only one way to solve these little problems: to have the mind of Christ. Think about this carefully. Here was the ablest mind in the church, meeting the simplest problem in the church and not being equal to it! It was as if Einstein were stumped by the simplest problem in arithmetic. The people said, "When Paul comes, or writes, he will solve our little difficulties. The solution is the mind of Paul." Paul, however, said, "The solution is the mind of Christ."

Imagine! This is the same Paul who, before his conversion, believed firmly that what organized religion needed was *his* mind. So he had studied, become a Pharisee, persecuted the Nazarenes, and meticulously observed the law. No doubt his elders and his peers both thought of him as the Pharisee most likely to succeed. How fortunate they were to have such a brilliant and rising star on their side! But notice how, after his conversion, Paul said to the church at Philippi, as it faced its little problems, "You don't need me and my mind, but Christ and His."

It makes sense. The church is the body of Christ. Shouldn't the body of Christ, then, have the mind of Christ? To be sure. And when it doesn't have the mind of Christ, what, then, does it become?

Did you ever read the story of Frankenstein? It is properly labeled a horror story. A scientist creates a body, but somehow his creation gets a mind of its own, whereupon it becomes a monster, destroying everything, including itself and its creator. But isn't this what has happened all too often in the church? Whenever the body of Christ does not have the mind of Christ, you have a monster. And there has been bloodshed and war throughout history to prove this point. There are few things more to be feared, perhaps, than the body of Christ that doesn't have the mind of Christ. For then, by some strange alchemy from hell, beyond my abilities to explain, it all turns into anti-Christ.

So when Paul told the body of Christ in Philippi to have the mind of Christ, he was saying something we do well to hear. He was telling them to lose their minds, as he had lost his, and acquire Christ's.

What is Christ's mind? Paul describes it later in the same chapter: ". . . who, though he was in the form of God, did not count equality with God a thing to be grasped, but emptied himself, taking the form of a servant, being born in the likeness of men. And being found in human form he humbled himself and became obedient unto death, even death on a cross" (Philippians 2:6-8).

29

That is the mind of Christ. Paul was a man who lost his mind to gain a better one.

*   *   *   *   *

For pre-communion devotions, try pondering Philippians 2:1-8. It will help you and your fellow Christians to be one in Christ, a unity that is attained when all have His mind, and not their own.

4

THE MINNOW IS MAN

Circumcised the eighth day,
of the stock of Israel,
of the tribe of Benjamin,
a Hebrew born of Hebrews,
a Roman citizen,
brilliant, and educated. . . .

It is quite possible that with all these things going for him, Paul, when his name was still Saul, was a rather insufferable sort. What evidence there is seems to support this notion. It may even be that this is something of what he had in mind when he wrote, "When I was a child, I spoke like a child, I thought like a child, I reasoned like a child" (1 Corinthians 13:11). For the young often think they have all the answers, and their parents none. Who was it who said that when he was sixteen he thought his father stupid, but was surprised when he was twenty-one to discover how much his father had learned?

Your problem, however, may be the reverse of Paul's. You are impressed, not with how much you know, but rather with how little you know, and how low your level of information is in matters pertaining to the faith. In fact, it is precisely this that holds you back from your commitment or makes you hesitate at the threshold of the upper room.

You will be interested to know, therefore, that on this point Paul, after his conversion, came over to your side. If before he met his Lord he knew all the answers or thought he did, he indicates that after his conversion he knew very few. For notice how in 1 Corinthians 13:9 and 12 he says, not once, but twice, that we "know in part."

Incidentally, this subject of knowledge is a continuation of our previous chapter. The emphasis there on the mind of Paul may have intimidated you. It seems a rather good idea at this point, therefore, to remain with the subject a bit longer. For a brief while let us consider the measure of anybody's knowledge, including Paul's. Is it great or is it small?

In my work as a pastor I make frequent visits to the sick in hospitals. As often as I make these calls, I stand amazed at the wonderful progress man has made in the field of medicine. The operating rooms might more aptly be labeled miracle rooms. Patients come and many of them find amazing healing and restoration to health. "Sensational" is a word we ought to use sparingly and with discretion. But such are the developments and the accomplishments in the field of the healing arts that we are justified in using not only the word "sensational" but other words of equal strength. Surveying the strides of medical science, we are led to conclude that man knows a lot. But when we see death approaching a patient, defying all man's skill to hold it off and claiming still another body despite all the doctors know to do, we sigh and say "We know so little."

Or, go to a university campus and see all the buildings and departments. There are the schools of law, dentistry, agriculture, engineering, physics, biology, and all the rest. The visitor is overwhelmed and concludes that man's knowledge is immense. Yet, as we see the university faculty assembled and hear its pronouncement that the area of man's ignorance far exceeds the area of his knowledge, we are driven to an opposite conclusion.

Again, enter a library where the many shelves are piled high with books in every language and on every subject. Survey the cards in the index file as they refer to authors and subjects from Archeology to Zoology, and from Archimedes to Zola and Zwingli, and you will be impressed with the accumulation of man's knowledge through the ages. The very size of the library of humankind suggests that we know a lot. Yet, one look into the deepest philosophy book on the shelf and we gather from the guesses and the soft speeches and the many inferences that our knowledge is not as vast as man's mountain of books would suggest.

So we can continue: We go to the moon — how

smart we are! Yet we seem incapable of beating our swords into plowshares (Isaiah 2:4) — how stupid we are! One side of the coin says we know a lot. The other side says we know but little. Some maintain that man's great knowledge may yet grow to total comprehension in some future century, while others maintain that, basically, man knows less today than he did a thousand years ago. Indeed, man knows nothing at all.

Which is right? Very likely neither. Paul would disagree with both extremes. Instead, as he said after his conversion, we know just a little. "We know in part."

It is in this connection that he spoke in 1 Corinthians 13:12 about seeing "in a mirror dimly." It is important, of course, to understand that word "mirror" as it was then understood. Mirrors today are practically perfect. We see clearly in them. But it was not always so. I can remember that when I was a boy, some mirrors were really quite bad because of imperfections in the glass. But even these were good, compared to those of Paul's day, which were usually made of burnished brass or polished silver, thus giving far poorer service than their modern counterparts.

Now what Paul said about knowledge was that we can see lines, but not clearly. We can recognize images, yet often the details are blurred, like in the mirror of his day. In short, we know a little. We know in part. So you can feel more comfortable now, impressed as you are with how little you know, seeing that Paul is alongside you in all of this.

So am I. Don't let preachers and theologians fool you or frighten you when they use big words and preach long sermons. The truth is that we don't know very much either. There was a period in church history, known as the period of Scholasticism, when the ministers and professors were tempted to construct theological systems of intellectual completeness. They began filling in the gaps of knowledge everywhere, in order to make all things plain. But their systems were not very plain, and not at all true. The scholastics forgot what Paul said about God's judgments being unsearchable and His ways past finding out (Romans 11:33). They forgot what Paul said in 1 Corinthians 13 about our knowing just in part and seeing as in a mirror dimly. They forgot what Newton said shortly before his death: "I do not know what I may appear to the world, but to myself I seem to have been only a boy playing on the seashore and diverting myself in now and then finding a smoother pebble or a prettier shell than ordinary, while the great ocean of truth lay all undiscovered before me."

Perhaps Carlyle in *Sartor Resartus* said it best: "To the minnow every cranny and pebble and quality and accident of its little native creek may have become familiar. But does the minnow understand the ocean tides and periodic currents, the trade winds and monsoons and moon's eclipses, by all of which the condition of its little creek is regulated and may — from time to time — be quite overset and reversed? Such a minnow is man; his creek this planet Earth, his ocean the immeasurable all, his monsoons and periodic currents, the mysterious course of Providence through aeons of aeons."

A medical student goes to college and to medical school, and then returns. When he does, we discover that his knowledge of the human body is considerable. Another goes to college and then to a school of law. And he, too, upon emerging and setting up practice, reveals a brisk knowledge of such matters as state law, corporation law, criminal law, and the like. But the man who goes to seminary and returns knows considerably less in his field — though he may have applied himself more diligently to his studies — than the other two. He knows but little. This is not his fault, nor the seminary's fault. It's just, you see, that his subject is so very very big.

I have gone to seminary. Let me take a moment to reveal to you how little I know. Let me choose as a subject, "The Origin of Evil." Certainly this pertains to my field. It is a topic, however, that contains some deep and unanswerable problems. Evil emanates from Satan. But who made Satan? I may not say that God is the origin of evil: the Bible tells me that (James 1:13). When it comes to this subject, therefore, I can ultimately only shrug my shoulders and admit ignorance.

Or, take the often debated subject of "Divine Sovereignty and Human Responsibility." Again, this is a matter pertaining to my area. It is certainly biblical to hold to God's predestining and electing grace (Ephesians 1:5). Yet, it is equally biblical to say that man is responsible for his acts

(Luke 12:20,21). But how do you bring these two together? In the last analysis I can only say that I don't know, and that the difference is resolved in an intelligence higher than my own, or anyone's.

Or, take something quite different — like a funeral. This, too, is in my line. Why was this person taken and not that person over there? Why did this individual, so needed by others, get called away from earth? What, precisely, happens to the soul at the moment of its severance from the body? Can the departed see us? The questions I am asked when death has made a visit are varied and perplexing and beyond the reaches of my knowledge.

We could continue in this vein, but I think we have said enough. The point is plain. The minnow is man. We see in a mirror dimly. We know in part.

But wait. If we know in part, if we know only a little, then it follows that we do know something. It may not be much, yet something is always more than nothing. What, then, is that "little" that we know, that which Paul knew after his conversion had shrunk his head?

To find an answer, we must turn to the letter Paul wrote to the Roman Christians of years ago. Now I know that the Book of Romans seems a very formidable document. A few pages back we said that it stands as proof of the greatness of Paul's mind, and this is true. There is, however, another side to this coin. For the reader to conquer this book, he must divide it. Doing this, we discover three divisions, whose listing represents, in fact, the sum of Paul's little knowledge.

The first section of Romans deals with the subject of the sinfulness of man. Discarding his plume of pedigree entirely, Paul says in Romans 3:22,23 that ". . . there is no distinction; since all have sinned and fallen short of the glory of God."

The second part of the book deals with the topic of salvation. In the fifth chapter, the sixth verse, he writes, "While we were yet helpless, at the right time Christ died for the ungodly." And in that marvelous eighth chapter, he writes, in the first verse, "There is therefore now no condemnation for those who are in Christ Jesus."

The third part of Paul's letter to the Roman Christians deals with the life of thankfulness and service to God that Christians must live in their gratitude for salvation. In the opening verses of the twelfth chapter he says, "I appeal to you therefore, brethren, by the mercies of God, to present your bodies as a living sacrifice, holy and acceptable to God, which is your spiritual worship. Do not be conformed to this world, but be transformed by the renewal of your mind, that you may prove what is the will of God, what is good and acceptable and perfect."

Here was the sum total of the knowledge of Paul. Years later, two men were to write a catechism in Heidelberg, Germany. In composing it, Ursinus and Olevianus followed this schema of the Book of Romans (Sin, Salvation, Service). "What three things must you know?" they wrote.

Their answer was: "First, how great my sins and misery are; the second, how I am delivered from all my sins and misery; the third, how I am to be thankful to God for such deliverance."

I remember the time I attended a service of worship in a large state penitentiary (happily as a visitor and not a prisoner). The men filed in with expressions revealing something less than enthusiasm. Their faces fell even lower when the chaplain, a somewhat scholarly looking gentleman, told them that he was going to reveal to them the full extent of his great knowledge. The captive audience brightened considerably, however, when the speaker revealed the fact that this would take less than five minutes. The clergyman, thereupon, proceeded to tell them all he knew; namely, that they were sinners and needed a Saviour, for whom they should live lives in accordance with His wishes and desires.

The sum and substance of Paul's knowledge was the same. It was but little. Yet, the little he knew was, in fact, a lot; enough to live on; enough to die on. A little knowledge, Alexander Pope said, is a dangerous thing. But the "little knowledge" that was Paul's is a blessed thing. It may not be much, but it is enough. And because it is enough it is a lot.

* * * * *

Read 1 Corinthians 13:9-13. To be a communicant, you need not be a seminary graduate. Instead, and in keeping with 1 Corinthians 13:13, let there be an emphasis in your heart on Christ's love for you, yours for Him, and yours for your neighbor.

THE SPUR OF NECESSITY

Some people have the happy facility of losing themselves in hobbies, projects, or special interests. I well remember such an individual, some years back, who developed an overwhelming interest in tropical fish. Soon there were fish in every corner of every room in his house. Anglers catch fish, but in this case it was the other way around. Later this person developed a similar passion for music records and hi-fi equipment, immersing himself as completely in this hobby as he had drowned himself earlier in the aerated waters of his aquariums. Still later, it was all roses and chrysanthemums. Meanwhile, some of his friends who watched amusedly were not able to develop any deep interests on their own. Instead they fell asleep nightly before their television sets. "Surely," I thought, "these, though laughing at the man in question, are the poorer, not being able to muster such intensities of interests in anything or anyone outside themselves."

Greater than complete devotion to a hobby, however, desirable as this may be, is the giving of oneself with equal intensity to the Christian faith. Such a man was Martin Luther. Zeal for his Lord consumed him when he spoke his famous words before the Diet of Worms: "Here I stand. I can do no other." He was reminiscent of Peter, another captive soul, who years before, standing before a similar body, had said, "We cannot but speak of what we have seen and heard" (Acts 4:20).

Paul, too, was this sort of person. In 1 Corinthians 9:16, he wrote, "For necessity is laid upon me. Woe to me if I do not preach the gospel." With these words, he was saying that he had to do what he was doing, and he had to do it with all his might.

But, come to think of it, when was necessity not laid on Paul? He was always a driven man. By constitution, like the man with the roses, Paul could never do anything by halves. This young man, so highly born that he was circumcised the eighth day, of the stock of Israel, of the tribe of Benjamin, a Hebrew born of Hebrews, a citizen of Rome, and so gifted with a mind that he became the great Gamaliel's greatest protégé, was not much inclined to become a playboy. He was not about to go off into some foreign country and there spend himself in riotous living as a prodigal. Nor was he interested in just living a comfortable life.

This is the affliction of some, to be sure. This is

the disease, in fact, that holds many within its grip today. Like Paul, we live in a great time of history. The issues are big, and the challenges are large, even as they were two thousand years ago. There's work to be done, there's need for men of muscle who will bend their backs and shoulder burdens and give themselves without worrying about being rewarded. We cannot say this without at the same time asking heaven for more men and women who will be equal to the day, and less of those whose only interest is the job with the best retirement plan.

See Paul then; with birth, brains, and drive. On what would he expend his boundless energy? Where was there a cause that would consume him and burn him up, if necessary? Where, in all this world, was there something that would challenge every inch of his able mind, in the service of which he could say, "So what, if I am consumed! Just so I do this thing."

"A good question," countless would say today. "Where, indeed, do you find such a thing? Let me know when you do find it, though, personally, I don't think you will." The French philosopher Jean-Paul Sartre writes: "This is really the biggest joke of all — that a man should be an animal capable of living for a cause! But there is, not anywhere, a cause to find. Man has a heart to give, yet nothing and no one in all the universe to give it to. This is the cruellest pain of all."

We must take issue, however, with Sartre. There is, indeed, a cause. There are, in fact, two causes to which you can give yourself. Either of these two causes, furthermore, will challenge you right down to the ground, and take all you have to give and more.

To present these causes here in the best possible way, I shall attempt to draw a picture of one of the more dramatic scenes to be found in the entire Bible. I refer you to the time in the early church when the number of disciples multiplied rapidly making the apostles extremely busy. Seven men were selected to render them assistance, specifically, to tend to the ministration of the poor (Acts 6:3).

Among the seven selected, there was a young man by the name of Stephen, an individual who was in the grip of Jesus Christ. He had given himself to his Lord, who he knew had given Himself to him. Nor was his gift of self a partial one. He had joined the Christian movement all the way. The Bible says that Stephen was full of the Holy Spirit, full of wisdom, full of faith, and full of power (Acts 6:8,10; 7:55). There was nothing "halfway" about the man.

As a matter of fact, this individual was so wholly dedicated and so completely committed that when a committee of the church came to call to see if he would be willing to serve the church in some special way, they found a ready listener. They did not offer him so high a role as that of an apostle. In truth, what they offered him was a position much lower, involving much work and little glory. "We need some men to take care of the poor," they said. "We need some assistants to wait on tables, and to do a host of detail work in order to release the apostles for their greater tasks." They offered Stephen no glamor. They would not have blamed him had he demurred and refused. But he responded in the affirmative. Along with several others like him, he went to work in order that the apostles might devote themselves "to prayer and to the ministry of the word" (Acts 6:4).

Stephen was so wholly dedicated that, besides the work that was his to do, he started preaching too. Just as he gave himself completely to his assigned tasks, so he devoted himself unreservedly to that which was over and above his line of duty. As was bound to happen whenever anyone showed such zeal for the Christian faith, the opposition arose, even though, as the Bible says, "They could not withstand the wisdom and the Spirit with which he spoke" (Acts 6:10). Unable to find grounds for convicting Stephen, his opponents obtained false witnesses who accused Stephen of blasphemy (Acts 6:11). A trial was held, and at this trial Stephen spoke. His speech has been preserved for us in Acts 7. It is generally referred to as Stephen's apology. It happens to be about the best sermon in the whole book, and it was delivered by one who was not even a preacher. You know what took place after the sermon. Stephen was taken outside the city and stoned till dead. As the executioners removed their cloaks, the better to throw the stones, they handed their coats to a youth named Saul (Acts 7:58).

Like Stephen, who at that moment was bleeding to his death, Saul, later named Paul, was also dedicated and full of loyalty to his cause, which, however, was the very opposite of Stephen's. Thus, in this picture, briefly sketched, we see two young men, equally dedicated, equally consecrated. Two young men with necessity laid on both of them; one for Christ, and one against Him.

All of this brings us back to the complaint of many a modern person who stands rootless on the earth with, he says, nothing to which he can give his life. The truth of the matter, however, is that there is a cause. There are, in fact, two causes that will take all a man has to offer: the one is Christ, the other is anti-Christ. In Acts 7 we see both portrayed. There is Stephen wholly given to the one and Paul wholly given to the other. One is interested in promoting Christ and saving all His enemies; the other in stopping Christ and killing all His friends.

These two causes are still with us today. The cause of anti-Christ is represented, for example, by present-day atheistic communism. Believe me, its followers find "necessity laid upon them." They are aggressive for their cause and constrained by their philosophy. They cannot help speaking the things they have seen and heard. Their call to others is loud and clear. "Do you want a cause? Do you wish to give yourself to something big? Then join our band. You will be given work to do. You will begin by just holding our coats, but you'll end up, when ready, with rocks in your hands to cast against those who have rocks in their heads, whom we seek to liqui-date and destroy." This is the cause of anti-Christ. It is of a piece with the cause of Saul in Acts 7.

But there is also Stephen and the cause of Christ. This cause is also so big it will simply claim all of you, as it did with Stephen not only, but with Augustine, Luther, Calvin, Knox, Whitefield, Wesley, and a host of others.

It is a tragic shame that there are those who say they are of the church on whom, however, no such "necessity" seems to be laid. It must be that their hearts harbor deficient conceptions of the gospel, thus accounting for their lukewarm tem-peratures. John Calvin complained about this already in his day. He observed that there were some preachers who counted aggressiveness as un-becoming to their station.

I say, however, that when "necessity" is laid on you, it is a spur that makes placidity an im-possibility. Can a man enter fully into the Chris-tian faith and be silent? Can there be a response to the gospel that is not complete? What a thing it is that there are those within the camp of Christianity — the greatest cause in all the world and in all of history — who are not moved to full response, remaining mere onlookers at the cele-bration of the sacrament. Not getting into the faith heart and soul, they miss the joy and blessing.

Paul held coats at the stoning of Stephen, already wishing that he was big enough to throw the stones. Persecuting the church a little later, he was a Pharisee in zeal. The Lord looked down and said that He could use that man for Himself, and when that happened, Paul became as dedicated in the one camp as he had been in the other. Before his conversion he said, "Necessity is laid on me." After his turning, he said it even more intensely. In a day of primitive transportation, he traversed both land and sea. We see him in a tiny ship without modern means of navigation, tossed about by the mighty Mediterranean, and we ask, "what is he doing there?" We notice him setting out from Tarsus at sea level to climb the mountain passes, trudging wearily through the rock gorge called the Cilician gates, some 4,300 feet in altitude, all the while bearing his handicap, his thorn in the flesh, and we wonder, "what motivates him?" Listen to him as he writes to the Corinthians: "Five times I have received at the hands of the Jews the forty lashes less one. Three times I have been beaten with rods; once I was stoned. Three times I have been shipwrecked; a night and a day I have been adrift at sea; on frequent journeys, in danger from rivers, danger from robbers, danger from my own people, danger from Gentiles, danger in the city, danger in the wilderness, danger at sea, danger from false brethren, in toil and hardship, through many a sleepness night, in hunger and thirst, often without food, in cold and exposure" (2 Corinthians 11:24-27).

But why? Why should a man burdened with a physical weakness and unappreciated by so many embark on such formidable journeys? Why should a man start out from Jerusalem and point himself to the ends of the earth? What is his motive, and what is his cause? The answer, of course, is that Paul saw Jesus Christ and the need of the world. The answer is that he was a man who had to give himself to something, completely and unreservedly. This he did, before Damascus, but to the wrong cause. After Damascus, he found the right one, and so gave himself all the more. As a young man, he could not understand Stephen's necessity to preach Christ even while rocks were hurled at him. Years later, the man who held the coats of Stephen's murderers, had the mantle of Stephen himself fall on him.

Stephen died. Necessity was laid on him to stand for Christ; but he died. Paul, shifting camps and causes by the grace of God, took Stephen's place and did the same. Paul died too. Thereupon, others who had necessity laid on them filled his vacancy. And so on, to the present day, to you. Is necessity also laid on you to stand for the Lord? Do you feel its spur? There are those who are of anti-Christ today, with all their soul and mind and strength. Can you match them? But, for the Saviour, not against? Consistently, not just temporarily like the man who shifted his allegiance from tropical fish to chrysanthemums? It is really only by way of losing yourself wholly, in the cause of the Christian commitment, that you will, like Paul, find yourself.

*   *   *   *   *

No one should go to the table of the Lord without confessing the sin of harboring a lukewarm,

49

tepid heart for the Master. It is good to read Revelation 3:14-18, taking encouragement from verse 19, especially the first four words.

6

THE BRIDGE OF SIGHS

In Cambridge, England, St. John's College spans the river Cam with an enclosed bridge built in 1826 and known as the Bridge of Sighs. It is named after a more ancient and more famous structure in Italy which links the Doge's Palace with the jail in Venice. Here prisoners who were sentenced to their deaths crossed over, dejected in mind and heart. Hence the name. Presumably, students at St. John's cross their bridge with equal dejection as they make their way to their examinations, which are, to them, not entirely unlike executions.

There is another Bridge of Sighs. It reaches from man to his creator, and carries the sorrows of the former to the throne of the latter. David crossed it ("against Thee, Thee only have I sinned . . ." — Psalm 51:4), though he was by no means the first and certainly not the last. Not a foot bridge, it is crossed only by those who crawl on their knees. All who do this are noticed instantly by God.

To prove this, we need only to turn to Acts 9:11, where we read, "Behold, he is praying." When people explore the sights of some new place or country together, the travelers are constantly drawing one another's attentions to the wonders that fill their eyes. "Look!" they cry as new views come into focus. "See the canyon." "Look at that mountain." Similarly, God. When a man finally bows before Him in penitent prayer, He calls the attention of the angels and men on earth.

It is in this spirit of excitement that Acts 9:11 must be read. Paul was on his knees. He lay prone on the Bridge of Sighs. "And the Lord said unto Ananias, 'Rise and go to the street called Straight, and inquire in the house of Judas for a man of Tarsus named Saul; for behold [look!], he is praying' " (Acts 9:11). It is necessary at this point to allow the eye, perusing this page of the Bible, to skip ahead to part of the seventeenth verse as well. "So Ananias departed and entered the house. And laying his hands on him [Paul], he said, 'Brother. . . .' "

This is nothing less than holy ground. It is a place where we move on tiptoe. There is a sense in which, at this point, I should stop writing and you should stop reading, for here is a picture worth a thousand words that might be spoiled with one. If you ask me, "What is the gospel all about — and don't go on and on about it, but give it to me short and in a nutshell," then I give you this scene from the pages of the Holy Scriptures. It is that of a man on his knees in darkness. He knows that he has sinned, unspeakably and shamefully. Then Jesus walks in through the door, places his hand on the shoulder of the sinner, and says, "Brother."

This was a meeting on the Bridge of Sighs between Christ and Paul. They had met at least twice before. Let us look at those two earlier meetings.

The first time these two met was in Jerusalem. It was on the occasion of the execution of the first martyr of the church, a deacon whose name was Stephen, whom we met in the previous chapter. To recapitulate just briefly, this young man was full of grace, and power and faith. Necessity was laid upon him to preach the gospel of salvation through Jesus Christ. Furthermore, he accompanied his words with great signs and wonders (Acts 6:8), though we don't exactly know what these signs and wonders were. For all of these activities, he was seized and brought before the council where, we can assume, Paul was also present as a viewer and a witness. Consider what took place then:

1: They looked on Stephen's face "as if it were the face of an angel" (Acts 6:15).
2: They listened to a sermon delivered by this deacon.
3: Cut to the heart, they reacted by grinding their teeth in fury. They plugged their ears, rushed upon Stephen and, dragging him outside the city, they pelted him with stones (Acts 7:58).

4: They heard a bleeding Stephen cry, "Lord Jesus, receive my spirit" (Acts 7:59).

5: They heard his further words: "Lord, do not hold this sin against them" (Acts 7:60).

I submit to you that these five steps constituted Paul's first meeting with Jesus Christ. Let us consider them again.

1: Paul was looking upon Stephen's face as if it were the face of an angel. This, incidentally, is the way it ought always to be when one of the world meets one who is of Christ. Paul sensed there was something different about this man. He did not know its nature exactly and precisely, and he could not define it in whole or part. But there was something about this Stephen that reminded him of angels and not devils; of heaven instead of hell.

I say again, this is the way it ought to be whenever the world meets a Christian. Sadly, this is not always so. Christians do not always leave the best impressions. The Revised Standard Version says that they "gazed at him" (Acts 6:15). The King James Version says that they "looked steadfastly on him." So others always do with Christians and the Christian church. What they see, sometimes, is more reminiscent of devils than angels. But Stephen was a faithful representative of Christ. When Paul and the others fastened their eyes on him, they had to admit that looking on Stephen was like looking up — not down. In this way, then, Paul, through Stephen, met Jesus Christ.

2: All those who were present that day, including Paul, heard a Christ-centered sermon (Acts 7). To this we need only add that anyone who hears one message presenting the Saviour as the Saviour has, according to God's word, met the Saviour.

This is why it is so important that all messages from church pulpits be Christocentric. As a preacher, I remind myself of this point regularly. After all, one never knows who may be present in the congregation; some Paul, perhaps, who has not yet turned and changed.

In the pulpit of my church there is a small plaque for every preacher who occupies this pulpit to read. Its words, taken from John 12: 21, are a great reminder: "Sir, we would see Jesus." It is only when such a request is heeded, that what purports to be a sermon actually becomes a sermon.

Undoubtedly, you have your heroes, as I have mine. One of mine is Thomas Chalmers, whose statue is in Edinburgh, Scotland. Chalmers was a mighty pulpiteer of years gone by whose messages, filled with knowledge and erudition, were heard by people who came from miles away. He did not, however, present the Saviour. One Sunday morning as this great and learned clergyman mounted his pulpit, his mind filled with the pearls of wisdom he had prepared for an overflowing congregation, he opened the massive pulpit Bible to discover that someone had secretly and anonymously inserted a message on a slip of paper at the

Bible lesson for the day. It simply quoted the words cited above: "Sir, we would see Jesus." This incident, unnoticed by the congregation, marked his turning point to the preaching of the true gospel of the Scriptures. Shortly thereafter Chalmers preached his famous sermon, still remembered, entitled "The Expulsive Power of a New Affection."

Stephen, presumably, had not gone to seminary. All the same, he knew what made a sermon a sermon. Thus, all who listened, Paul included, met Jesus Christ, who was the theme of Stephen's every sentence.

3: The audience that day, we said, ground their teeth with fury and plugged their ears. Paul as well. And it is no wonder when you consider a portion of what Stephen said. Imagine Paul, who was not only circumcised, but on the eighth day to boot, being classified as among the uncircumcised (Acts 7:51). Listen further: "You always resist the Holy Spirit. As your fathers did, so do you. Which of the prophets did not your fathers persecute? And they killed those who announced beforehand the coming of the Righteous One, whom you have now betrayed and murdered, you who received the law as delivered by angels and did not keep it" (Acts 7:51-53).

I recall the story of a minister who, of a Sunday morning, addressed his fashionable congregation in the following manner: "Earlier this morning I addressed the prisoners at the county jail. Now I speak to men and women of wealth and station. The only difference between my earlier hearers and the present ones is that they are behind bars whereas you are not."

Those words had bite. So did Stephen's. By these too Paul encountered Christ. It was as if Jesus was looking at the life of Paul through these words and saying to him that it was a life that fell far short.

4: They heard a bleeding Stephen cry: "Lord Jesus, receive my spirit" (Acts 7:59).

5: The last words of the first Christian martyr that fell upon the ears of Paul were: "Lord, do not hold this sin against them" (Acts 7:60). Both of these utterances were reminiscent of those spoken by the Saviour from a cross. Stephen spoke Christ's language, as all Christians must. In these, also, Paul met the Master.

Everything about this meeting with Stephen—what he said and did and how he looked — was for Paul his first meeting with his Lord. Others may meet Christ as well — through us.

What was Paul's reaction? I wish, of course, that I could tell you that he yielded and that he gave himself. What a lot of misery there could have been avoided, for others as well as Paul, had he capitulated to his Lord on the occasion of this first confrontation. But Paul resisted; and in consequence he found no peace on the road ahead. Instead of surrendering, Paul did the very opposite. The Bible tells us that he approved of Stephen's murder (Acts 8:1).

He did more. Paul responded to this first meeting with Christ by way of violent reaction. He breathed "threats and murder" (Acts 9:1). "He laid waste the church, and entering house after house, he dragged off men and women and committed them to prison" (Acts 8:3). This, to say it again, was the awful result of the first meeting between Paul and Christ. I say this again, because you can't understand Paul on the Bridge of Sighs, in the house of Judah, in the city of Damascus, unless you remember this.

But let us go on to the second meeting that took place between these two. I have tried to explain the first one, but it is impossible to analyze the second. We know the circumstances, but hardly more. Paul applied for, and received permission to extend his campaign against the followers of the Nazarene (Acts 9:1,2). Accordingly, he set out with his retinue for the city of Damascus. It was a road he chose and, as it turned out, the last one he ever chose all by himself. It was on that road that the second meeting, so different from the first, took place. A bright light surrounded him, and a voice as well, saying, "Why do you persecute me? I am Jesus whom you are persecuting" (Acts 9:4,5). His traveling companions also heard, though they saw no one (Acts 9:7). Paul, tall and proud, and wearing his plumes of pride, was unhorsed. He fell to the ground, blinded, with those words ringing in his ears: "I am Jesus," meaning Saviour (Matthew 1:21). No wonder, when those words sank in, he neither ate nor drank for three days straight.

If I had been present, I am sure that I would

not have been able to describe the scene to you. When we speak of God or of His appearances we stammer. When it comes to the things that pertain to this we are, said Martin Luther, "like young children learning to speak, and using only half and quarter words." Whenever Paul sought to reduce this great decisive experience in his life to articulation, he found all his resources of language inadequate. Striving as he did, he never really found the words adequate to communicate this deep experience. It could not be spoken, and so he employed the word "unspeakable" (2 Corinthians 9:15).

Some time later, Paul described this second meeting with his Lord in a way that captured something of its splendor. Writing in 2 Corinthians 4:6 he referred back to the beginning of the Book of Genesis: ". . . it is the God who said, 'Let light shine out of darkness,' who has shone in our hearts. . . ." Here he likened the conversion experience, his own included, to that moment in creation when God said, "Let there be light" (Genesis 1:3). It was as if he said, "Before Damascus, I was without form and void, and darkness lay upon me. Yet all the while, the Spirit of God was brooding upon me, through Stephen, and in a host of other ways. Then God said, 'Let there be light'; and there was, thereupon, a miracle of birth, and light, with order, and purpose, and beauty to follow; the beginning of eternal day and the ending of chaos and ancient night."

For the rest of his life, Paul was under the impress and influence of that appearance of his

Lord to him. He never forgot it. It lay forever after in the forefront of his consciousness. It was far and away the most vital and formative influence in his life. Compared to it, everything else — his Hebrew ancestry, his rabbinic training, his Hellenistic contacts, and every factor of heredity and environment — was completely secondary. It was no fantasy. This was no autosuggestion on his part. "He appeared unto me," he said to the Corinthians (1 Corinthians 15:8). "I have seen Christ!", he indicated to the Galatians (Galatians 1:16).

There is a question that must be asked at this point. I am sure you have had, like Paul, the first meeting with the Christ. You have met Him through sermons, perhaps, preached by those who stand in St. Stephen's tradition, or through the less formal witness of some friend. But have you, again, like Paul, had that second encounter? It need not be as dramatic or as sudden. There are those who have listened to Stephens all their lives who have yet to come to that second kind of meeting in which, yielding themselves completely, they say, "Lord, what wilt thou have me to do?" (Acts 9:6 — KJ).

But let us now go to a brief consideration of a third meeting between the Nazarene and the man of Tarsus. It cannot be understood except in the light of the other two. In the journey of a soul from self to Christ, there must be that first encounter when the name of the Lord is heard, and the second when the Spirit overpowers. But there must also be a third, when a man, stricken in his heart and soul, falls upon his knees. In that position, he neither eats nor drinks — but prays. "O Lord, be merciful to me . . . I am not worthy . . . Sins of youth remember not . . . I am the chief of sinners . . . Answer and give pardon."

When the blind Paul petitioned in this manner, he heard the opening of a door and footsteps on the floor. And he heard a voice. It was not unkind and harsh. The words were not such words as he seemingly might have expected. "So you are Paul of Tarsus. The high and mighty one! Yet not so mighty now, I see. Tell me, how many Christians did you persecute and kill? And how many did you cause to tremble in the darkness as you are trembling in the darkness now? Perhaps you'd better sit here for a while. Perhaps, if you refrain from wickedness henceforth, I'll find some employment for you, like tying and untying both my sandals" (John 1:27).

No, these were not the words he heard. Instead, there was a gentle hand on his shoulder. It was really the Master's hand. And there was a gentle voice. It was really the Master's voice. And the voice said, "Brother" (Acts 9:17).

This was the third meeting between Paul and Christ. Sadly, a second meeting does not always follow the first, but a third always follows the second.

In Venice, we said, there is a link between the Doge's Palace and the jail, known as the Bridge of Sighs. Here, prisoners who were sentenced to their deaths crossed over, dejected in mind and heart. Hence the name.

There is another Bridge of Sighs that reaches from man to man's creator, and carries the sorrows of the former to the throne of the latter. But all who cross this Bridge of Sighs, like Paul, find forgiveness, not condemnation.

*   *   *   *   *

In preparing for communion, it is good to breathe the words of the general confession, found in the Book of Common Prayer:

> "Almighty and most merciful Father; We have erred, and strayed from Thy ways like lost sheep. We have followed too much the devices and desires of our own hearts. We have offended against Thy holy laws. We have left undone those things which we ought to have done; and we have done those things which we ought not to have done; and there is no health in us. But Thou, O Lord, have mercy upon us, miserable offenders. Spare Thou them, O God, which confess their faults. Restore Thou them that are penitent; According to Thy promises declared unto mankind in Christ Jesus our Lord. And grant, O most merciful Father, for His sake; that we may hereafter live a godly, righteous, and sober life, To the glory of Thy holy Name. Amen."

7

ARABIAN NIGHTS AND
TARSUSIAN DAYS

Quite a few years ago, now almost beyond recall, Charles Sheldon's *In His Steps* was a bestseller everywhere. The author presented the thesis that every decision in life ought to be made in the light of "what would Jesus do?" He maintained that this question, posed before every situation and challenge, would serve as the Christian's unerring guide and measure.

I had a professor in seminary who maintained that this was wrong. "What Jesus might do in any given situation would not always be what you should do in a similar circumstance, because Christ is God and you are not." This distinction registered with me. "So," he continued, "the question to ask yourself is not, 'What would Jesus do?' but rather 'what would Jesus have me to do?'"

This was the very question Paul asked on the Damascus Road. Felled and blinded by the light, with the words of Christ still ringing in his ears, he stammered and said, "Lord, what wilt Thou have me to do?" (Acts 9:6 KJV).

We all assume — much too easily I think — just what it was that Jesus wanted Paul to do. If I asked you this question, I imagine you would say something like "Jesus wanted Paul to get himself turned around and start preaching the gospel." You might further point out to me that this is indeed what happened. Paul fought the church. Then, changing in heart, he began preaching Christ instead of fighting Him.

This, I think, is the picture most people have in their minds. Paul opposed the church. He was converted. He began preaching. Just like that. But the fact is that it wasn't *just like that* at all. Have you ever noticed in your reading of the Book of Acts how Paul drops out of the picture for a while? You don't read about him anymore in the last half of chapter nine. You don't read about him in all of chapter ten, nor in chapter eleven, except at the very last. For eighty-five verses in a row in Acts, you don't hear of Paul at all. There is a story behind this.

"Lord, what wilt Thou have me to do?" Paul thought it was to preach the gospel. Thus, after Ananias had come to him, he arose to the task. But it was all a bit premature. Though the people were amazed and confounded, they were also set on edge against him. The Holy Spirit — to put it another way — did not seem to bless his work with fruit.

So, we gather, and Paul did too, that his time

for preaching had not yet come, if it ever would. He was unripe and he was unready, a fact which, humanly speaking, allows me to give easier credence to this whole episode in his life. It sort of takes this entire affair out of the realm of unreality. Paul's heart had been changed. No doubt about it. But his head needed to catch up a bit. For this, God ordained that he should have some time to think.

This, then, explains his dropping out of the picture for almost ninety verses. "Lord, what wilt Thou have me to do?" Part of the answer is found in the first chapter of the Epistle to the Galatians, a companion passage to Acts 9. Here we learn that Paul journeyed to Arabia where he remained for a considerable length of time in spiritual retreat. Moses, too, you recall, had such a time of spiritual preparation, as did Elijah, St. Francis in his sickness, and Luther in the monastery of Erfurt. Even Jesus had His thirty years and His forty days. So Paul. He too was in for a time of deepening and seasoning.

Did you ever think of this?

When a convert from outside the church comes into the fellowship of believers where all have been Christians from childhood on, his testimony is like a refreshing breeze for the members of the congregation. I must say, however, and I do so with considerable hesitation, that it has been my experience that some initiates who testify unceasingly and seemingly without drawing breath, sometimes create adverse reactions. If you are such a person, I pray most earnestly that this observation will not inhibit your enthusiasm. You should witness as you must. Still, I confess to an impulse, to which I have yielded on occasion, of advising some to testify initially a little less and to think a little more. The man who has quit smoking sometimes gives offense to those still captive to the weed by overbearing oversell. It is a human failing. I do not imply that this was descriptive of Paul in his newfound faith, though it may well have been. What I do say is that Paul and present-day converts, too, find their testimonies more effective the more they deepen themselves in the rich soil of the whole gospel truth. Accordingly, God saw to it that Paul went into a measure of seclusion for the maturing of his faith. He went, consequently, to Arabia. He witnessed there, to be sure. He was not silent when there was occasion to speak. But his Arabian nights held long thoughts and deep introspections. It is not difficult, perhaps, to imagine him there "examining himself" and his new knowledge.

When Paul finally left Arabia, he was a homing pigeon. Where should he go and where did he go but to Damascus, the place of his spiritual birth. But his excitement, engendered by his return to action, was shaded by his disappointment that during his absence, enmity towards him had not diminished, but in fact increased. If you are a fisherman, you know how it feels, having risen early, to arrive at the lake only to find the weather so adverse as to make angling impossible. As a would-be fisher of men, Paul experienced similar sensations. The time was not yet right. To put the whole thing in another way, the devil didn't get over it in a hurry when he lost one of his best men to Jesus Christ. So there developed the plot on his life, which Paul could only avoid by going over the wall (Acts 9:25) unceremoniously, in a basket, presumably with some loss of dignity. There he scampered through the trees and bushes. Imagine him there in the dark, outside Damascus, a highly gifted, talented man with a desire to do great things for his Saviour, but with nowhere to go and no place where he could fit.

God makes it hard sometimes.

And so, as we fit the pieces of the Books of Acts and Galatians together, Paul went to Jerusalem, his heart being pulled to the Christians there. Like seeking like, perhaps he thought of those words in Psalm 119:63: "I am a companion of all those that fear Thee, of those who keep Thy precepts." He went especially to see Peter. This may have been because Peter was the leader, or because the fisherman too had once, as Paul, hurt the Master through his denials. Whatever the reason, the man of mind went to meet the man of heart.

Paul's general reception in Jerusalem was something less than the kind of cheers the astronauts, for example, receive upon their return from space. Like Jesus his Lord before him, Paul came unto his own and his own received him not (John 1:11). Doors were closed and faces were averted. "They were all afraid of him, for they did not believe that he was a disciple" (Acts 9:26).

Paul must have had his moments at this turn of events. He might have harbored an impulse to breathe a pox on all Christians. The forgiveness found with the Master is not always characteristic of His followers. Paul, too, discovered this. Yet, however unjustifiable his reception, it was somewhat understandable. Paul had sorely tried the Christians in his earlier days. He was a man with a past, and a past is always difficult to escape.

That is something to bear in mind.

If you have wasted yourself, as the prodigal in the parable, in something called "riotous living," you will have a new heart upon accepting Christ, but no new body. If you have lied and cheated all your life, you will, in yielding to the Lord, receive a new name in heaven, though you will, for a time at least, retain the old one on earth among all those you have defrauded. We pray to God "Sins of youth remember not," and our petitions find a ready ear. But often the sins of youth remember us. Paul was a Christian, among Christians; but it was hard to find acceptance. The believers' behavior towards him was not defensible, but it was predictable.

There was one, in Jerusalem, who saved the day. Often, among God's people, there are to be found, here and there, souls that are bequeathed with an extra degree of perception and sensitivity. Such a person was Barnabas. He had a special place in his heart, it seems, for strangers and for underdogs. He was a friend of the friendless, a fact for which he was held in high regard. In Acts

4:36,37, we read that he had land that he sold, the proceeds of which he gave to the church to be used for distribution among the poor. This man, respected and honored by all, took Paul under his wing (Acts 9:27) and from under a cloud. Thus, he was given "entree." It seemed, therefore, that Paul was about to launch out on some real piece of work.

But again, he was doomed to disappointment. He spoke boldly (the word can also be translated "brashly" — Acts 9:29) in the name of the Lord against the Greeks. The latter, in reaction, sought to kill him. The Christians, therefore, advised Paul to leave (Acts 9:30). It was made plain to him that it would be better for the cause if he were not in their midst. His presence was hurting, rather than helping. No doubt these sentiments, gently conveyed, were, nevertheless, hard to receive. Who could measure Paul's despondency when again, it appeared, he could not be used. Would his mistakes and background always be a roadblock to greater service? Where would he go? Not Damascus and, certainly, not Arabia again; while as for Jerusalem, he could not remain. There is some irony in where he did go. We read in Scripture that the brethren sent him forth to Tarsus (Acts 9:30).

Back where he came from!

He had left his home town at a rather young age. Some scholars estimate that he was about forty-two years old when he returned. At this point in the Bible narrative Paul sinks from sight for quite a long time. The years passed. In Jerusalem and in Damascus some remembered him, but others, new Christians, had only heard of him. "I was unknown," wrote Paul later to the Galatians (Galatians 1:22). And with Paul in some other place, the church had respite and peace (Acts 9:31).

Where did Paul live while in the city of his birth? It may be sound conjecture, and no more than that, to guess that it was not in his parental home. His father, if still alive, was a Pharisee. If still persisting in his earlier ways, he would be bitterly disappointed with a son who had become a follower of the Nazarene. It is possible, therefore, that Paul lived on Tent Street, for in those days all of one trade congregated. There, presumably, he made tents. His father had been right. "Better learn a trade," he had said. "A man never knows when he needs it to fall back on." That's what Paul did.

For how long? Some Bible scholars say at least three years, while others guess as high as ten. "Lord, what wilt Thou have me to do?" And God answered, "Make tents." So his hands grew hard and unaccustomed to books and quills and parchment. Years later, in the letter to the Galatians, he made reference to his penmanship: "See with what large letters I am writing to you (not "how large a letter" as in the KJV) with my own hand" (Galatians 6:11). It was as if he meant to call attention to his lack of skill in handwriting. There was good reason for that lack: back in Tarsus Paul had worked on a lot of tents.

It seems altogether likely that, what with those

many Arabian nights and Tarsusian days, Paul's real ministry, of which we read in the Book of Acts, did not commence until he was around fifty years old. This is worthy of note in a day and age when preachers of such vintage are considered by some as "over the hill." It is sad and silly, yet true, that in some highly competitive ecclesiastical circles, ministers dye their hair. The blame goes to the churches, many of which insist on younger men for the young people, and financial drives, and the like. Those of the cloth and pew who consider a clergyman old at forty-five do well to remember that the most effective preacher the Lord ever had working for Him on this earth was given a rather late start. Missionary boards might also remember this.

Paul's transition from a five-star general in the army of anti-Christ to the greatest missionary the church has ever had, was no overnight hocus-pocus. I always have great difficulty in believing the ex-drunkard who maintains that, after being on the bottle for twenty years, his burning, thirsting tongue was healed at the very moment of his conversion. I do not say it has not happened. God is certainly capable of bestowing cures that are instant and complete. But, for the comfort of those who, having come to Jesus Christ, are still wrestling with their weaknesses, I must point out that, for most, as we shall more clearly see in a later chapter, all struggles and problems do not end on the Damascus Road. The man who has lived a lustful life does not as a rule arrive immediately, upon conversion, to a mental state in

71

which his every thought is chaste and circum-
spect.

So it was with Paul. He had tasted nothing but
glory and success. Well-born, talented and heavily
endowed, he grew in pride. Thus, though on the
road to Damascus he had become a converted
man, he had still not reached the point where his
name was changed from Saul, meaning "the
welcome one," to Paul, meaning "the little one."
He was not arrogant in conversion. Still, there
was much in him that needed time, and thought,
and struggle.

God reduced Paul, and took His time about it,
as He so often does. As a young man Paul had
passed the tentmakers on Tent Street — on his
way to Jerusalem and a celebrated career. Seeing
them, he had probably thought their occupation
acceptable for them. As for him, he would climb
to higher heights. He came back, however, to
making tents, unnoticed, anonymous, unheralded.
"Lord, what wilt Thou have me to do?" And God
answered, "I'm going to make you a tradesman
in Tarsus."

It was during those Arabian nights, however,
and even more, those Tarsusian days, that Paul
grew in stature. As often as I read 1 Corinthians
13, that great treatise on love, or Romans 14, that
great passage on tolerance, I think of how long
and deeply this great persecutor must have dwelt
on these and other themes in those nights and
days of his retreat. Paul cannot be explained as a
Christian apart from the Damascus Road. He cannot be explained as a great theologian, mission-

ary, and man of spiritual breadth and stature apart from Arabia and his return to Tarsus.

"What wilt Thou have me to do, O Lord?" It took a while, but Paul found the light in the Old Testament Book of Micah (6:8) where we find the same question, plus the answer: "What doth the Lord require of thee but to do justly, and to love mercy, and to walk humbly with thy God."

This is what he really learned to do, in Arabia and in Tarsus. And it all gave deeper meaning to those words he was later to write: "I have learned," he said. What a lot was involved in those first three words! "I have learned, in whatever state I am, to be content" (Philippians 4:11).

*　　*　　*　　*　　*

"Mold me and make me
　After Thy will,
　While I am waiting,
　Yielded and still."

Regular devotions and "quiet times" are essential for the honing of the soul. Their absence can only impoverish the communion hour.

8

SACRED COWS

Though you may run across some four-footed and wild beasts, creeping things, and fowls of the air (Acts 10:12) in the next few pages, this chapter is not about animals, but about Paul. Pharaoh in the Old Testament had a dream about some ~~fat~~ *thin* cows eating ~~thin~~ *fat* cows (Genesis 41:1-45), a story that Joseph interpreted for him, landing himself the Prime Minister's job in Egypt. Joseph must have marveled sometimes when looking back on the involved and devious road unrolled by Providence that brought him to so high a place.

And Paul no less. There are parallels between his life and Joseph's. Both had auspicious beginnings and fond fathers. Both met with some reverses, even to the point of thinking that God had forgotten them. Both were heaven's choice to supply food for a starving world, though one brought physical, and the other spiritual food.

Both rose to their respective positions by way of some dreams about animals, though in Paul's case the visions were not his own, but Peter's (Acts 10:9ff.). Like the Old Testament Joseph before him, Paul must have reflected sometimes on the strange and wonderful design of heaven that had unfolded with the passing of his days. Perhaps these were his very thoughts when he wrote in Romans 8:28, "We know that all things work together for good to them that love God, to them who are the called according to his purpose."

With a two-thousand-year advantage in hindsight and perspective, we can trace some lines of the pattern for Paul better, perhaps, than he. Let us try, at any rate. God had said to Ananias in Damascus that "he [Paul] is a chosen instrument of mine to carry my name before the Gentiles . . ." (Acts 9:15). This is precisely what he was doing in his off-hours as a tentmaker in Damascus. There he was learning how to approach Greeks with the gospel. Yet this was only a preparation for what was to come.

At this same time Jerusalem was the center of the Christian church. Peter lived there, and James, no less a stalwart, and other leaders and apostles. The church was large, relatively speaking, and getting larger in the city of its birth. Meanwhile, there were also the dispersed Jewish Christians who lived in little knots, scattered all the way from here to there.

But there were some disadvantages to having Jerusalem serve as the capital of the Christian faith. The biggest, I suppose, was the fact that it was a place encrusted with tradition. For example, there was the temple, which so dominated the life and thought of all who lived in its environs. Just to mention one thing, there were all those daily offerings that were made within its walls. With Christ's sacrifice of Himself on the cross, such rituals were no longer necessary. Still, it was hard for the Christians in Jerusalem to wean themselves away from this practice of the centuries. Living within the shadow of the temple towers made this even more difficult.

I don't think we ought to be too hard on them on this account. We, too, find that changes do not come easily. Many of our own immediate forefathers gave strong resistance when some attempted to change the language of their church services to English. Battles were fought over changing from the common to the individual cup in the communion service. Some Roman Catholics are deeply unhappy over the fact that the mass has been transposed from Latin to their native tongue.

I recall a time when I was a visitor in a church of another denomination. Though Bible-centered, as my own, its customs and traditions were not the same. Communion was being celebrated on that particular day, and I had difficulty deciding whether to abstain, this being another church, or to participate, in which case I would ask for permission to attend. Settling on the latter of these two alternatives, I asked to see the pastor, who informed me that he was not empowered to grant me my request. Thinking, thereupon, that I had to see the elders or the church council who stood above him, he told me that they, no more than he, could grant me their consent.

Seeing that I was puzzled, the pastor smiled a kindly smile and explained: "The table is the Lord's table," he said, "it is not ours in any sense. If you belong to the Lord, you have every right to be present there. I cannot bar you from it, and even the 'permission' is not mine to give."

Coming, as I did, from a church whose procedure for visitors at communion services was designed to guard the table so that no one would eat and drink unworthily (1 Corinthians 11:29), I thought the pastor's position strange. I have since that day come to appreciate it deeply. At the time, however, my mind fastened on the difference in traditions, and the superiority of my own over his. Even now some who hold to "controlled" communion cannot understand the practitioners of "open," and vice versa.

So it is. Customs have the deepest roots, springing, as they do, from principles, real or imagined. "Open" communion might give spiritual indigestion to those who adhere to its stricter administration. And vice versa. Mahatma Gandhi, a vegetarian, had bad dreams when he ate meat; and the Mormon James Jesse Strang felt a stomach ache when he drank coffee. The Jewish Christians were no exception to this universal phenomenon, the more so because they lived in Templetown. It was not easy for them to break away from religious thought and worship patterns that had lasted through the centuries in the generations of their fathers.

Further, the Christians found it not only difficult to get out of the "offerings of animals" custom (Hebrews 10:1ff.), but equally hard to get into the "go ye into all the world" frame of mind (Matthew 28:19). It was not easy to think of Samaritans as people and not dogs (Matthew 15:26), to say nothing of reaching out to them in the love of Christ. And, when someone other than of the circumcision did attach himself to the church's ranks, it seemed downright wrong not to insist that he be conformed to all the ways of their fathers, including submission to the bloody rite. Clearly, therefore, something had to give if the church of Jesus Christ was ever to become truly Catholic instead of Jewish in its stamp and color.

At this point God communicated with Peter by means of a trance or vision that occurred three times. In it, the apostle was told to eat a meal including four-footed beasts, wild beasts, creeping things, and fowls of the air. Jews had been forbidden by ceremonial law to eat such food, so Peter demurred, saying that "unclean" meat had never passed his lips. But the voice that he heard said, "What God hath cleansed, that call thou not common" (Acts 10:15). The circumstances made the meaning quite apparent. When Peter related his vision to the Christians in Jerusalem, and the incident pertaining to Cornelius in connection with it, his fellow believers in

Jerusalem also got the message loud and clear. "Then to the Gentiles also God has granted repentance unto life," they said (Acts 11:18). But even so, their tendencies remained. It was hard to take Gentiles and not make them over into Jews. As a result, the mission program of the church had a hard time getting off the ground.

As has been said already, what was true then is also true today. Generally speaking, the last to accommodate itself to a new situation is the church. When history enters the twentieth century, the church is still, too often, in the nineteenth. It says, gathered round the Lord's table, that it looks forward to His return. The truth is, however, that oftentimes it is not only not forward looking, but equally unaware of the present. The church seems more often bent on preserving itself as it is and was, rather than accommodating itself to God's progression in history; a fact that, in every age, makes its younger members restive, impatient, and despairing.

The truth of the matter is that in the church of Jerusalem, and the church of every decade, there are too many sacred cows that need breaking, as the golden calf in the Old Testament wilderness needed smashing (Deuteronomy 9:21). In India, they impede progress less than in the church of Jesus Christ where they are worshipped too. I write not of cows of flesh and blood, but of old ways and methods and shibboleths, which, though once serviceable means to ends, have now become outdated ends in themselves. How often, in churches, changes are resisted on the grounds that "such things have never been done before." If you love the church, as I hope you do, you will not take exception to these remarks, seeing that they are made by one who shares in your affection. Criticism, proceeding from the right spirit, is generally better, though perhaps less pleasant, than blind love that slides over all shortcomings and imperfections.

The church whose goal is to preserve itself as it was, and is, when some forward motion is indicated, has a wrong goal. Though the church at Jerusalem was a wonderful one, it, nevertheless, had a bit of this deficiency. That is why God decided to change His base of operation. He had given His followers the great commission. He had underlined His universal outreach by way of Peter's vision, three times repeated. But though the believers understood, they still found themselves foisting Jewish ways on Gentile lives. So God shifted capitals from Jerusalem to Antioch. You can read all about it in the last half of Acts 11. Some of the dispersed, whom we mentioned earlier, were preaching Jesus Christ to the Gentiles, "and the hand of the Lord was with them, and a great number that believed turned to the Lord" (Acts 11:21).

Naturally, word concerning this development filtered back to Jerusalem. "Bad news travels fast," they say, but good news does too. When the Holy Spirit blesses the preaching of the gospel and moves the hearts of men to repentance and acceptance, the information gets around (Acts 11:22). The congregation at Jerusalem seems to have received the tidings, however, with a degree of caution, for which we cannot blame them. Accordingly, they decided to appoint one of their own members to have a look, and selected Barnabas for the investigation (Acts 11:22).

They could not have chosen a better man. If you should ever wish to make a Bible character a project for study, or name a child or a church after some saint, I would urge consideration of this man. The longer you look at him, the larger he looms. Had Jerusalem sent Peter, it is possible that he might have disapproved of many things he saw. Anybody else, too, after one look around might have said, "You're doing it all wrong. Back in Jerusalem we do it this way." But there were no barnacles on Barnabas. He was singularly unimpressed by sacred cows. "When he came and saw the grace of God, he was glad" (Acts 11:23a). Then "he exhorted them all to remain faithful to the Lord with steadfast purpose" (Acts 11:23b).

It is interesting to note how the sacred record stays with Barnabas for one more verse. "He was a good man," says Luke, among other things (Acts 11:24). Indeed, he was an excellent man. Not only did he react to the Antiochian scene as a man of vision would react, but it also occurred to him that he knew just the man, the right man, to work for Jesus Christ in this new setting. It was not someone back in Jerusalem, but another whom he had befriended some years before, a somewhat forgotten man. "So Barnabas went to Tarsus to look for Saul" (Acts 11:25).

We can only imagine the conversation that

81

transpired between them, or Paul's reaction when he was told that there was work for him in Antioch. Did he demur at first? Did he say he was too old for travel? Rather than conjecture, it is better to stay with the Bible narrative, which tells us that he went with Barnabas to Antioch, working side by side with this wonderful man in a growing vibrant situation (Acts 11:26).

The citizens of Antioch took note. In one of the pubs, two men talked about it over a flagon of wine and found another name for these followers of Christ — "Christians!" (Acts 11:26). In its earliest usage, it was a derisive term. It is still used by many in just this way.

I wonder what Jerusalem thought of all of these unfoldings? It seems they were no longer where the action was. Would they accept these new developments? Did they approve of Paul? Might there be a rift — a split — as the church was so often to experience in later years? It is interesting, in tracing the progression of the providence of heaven, to note two cementing, rather than fracturing, situations that unreeled themselves.

For one thing, the church in Jerusalem no longer enjoyed the peace that had dawned upon Paul's departure some years before. King Herod had inaugurated a persecution. He killed James and, imprisoning Peter, marked him for a similar fate (Acts 12). The other thing was the famine that brought great hardship to the Christians of Judea. The first development made persecution no longer a word synonymous with Paul, and the second gave the man of Tarsus, together with

Barnabas, the opportunity to come to his fellow believers in Jerusalem with relief in his hands (Acts 11:29,30). How strange and wonderful were the ways of God. Now Paul was literally taking Stephen's place in their midst, ministering to their physical needs, and suffering persecution along with them.

When their mission was accomplished, Barnabas and Paul returned to Antioch, joining the prophets and the teachers there (Acts 12:25). Acts 13:1 gives us the list: Barnabas (he is mentioned first), Simeon, Lucius, Manaen, and Paul (who is mentioned last). The Bible says that they were a spiritual lot. They fasted and prayed. They put first things first. Since their priorities were in proper order, the inevitable result was the development of a missionary spirit and program.

Mission-mindedness, you see, is never a hobby. One man likes fishing and another man plays chess. So, it sometimes seems, one church likes social work and another concentrates more on Christian education. There are psychological reasons as deep as the theological ones, that explain these realities. Sometimes it is as true of churches as it is true of individuals that one man's poison is another's cup of tea. But "mission" can never be placed in the classification of someone's hobby. This notion too is a sacred cow that needs to be annihilated. Outreach with the gospel to the ends of the earth is every church's calling, duty, and responsibility. Where true spirituality exists, this will be seen.

Such spirituality prevailed in Antioch. Therefore, the Christians wished to send forth two men. In answer to their prayers, the Holy Spirit said, "Set apart for me Barnabas" (Acts 13:2). Naturally. He was obviously qualified. "And Paul," the Spirit added.

Paul. Praise the Lord! So "they laid their hands on them and sent them off" (Acts 13:3). Thus began Paul's first missionary journey.

What a lot of intermingling providences lay behind Paul's ordination: his birth, his endowments, his training, his misdirected zeal, his conversion, his Arabian nights and Tarsusian days, and God's shift from Jerusalem to Antioch as a base of operations. Such guidance, so evident two thousand years ago from the perspective of the present, is still operative today. The same providence that led Paul to his task, leads you to God's upper room, and beyond, to service in His cause.

* * * * *

The communion administration varies from church to church, and from denomination to denomination. You may run into grape juice instead of wine; the common cup instead of the hygienic individual arrangement. You may kneel or stand, as the case may be; eat leavened bread or unleavened wafers. The elders serving may be men or, in some churches, women; the form elaborate or simple; the table open or closely supervised. Whatever the arrangements that may differ from your custom, don't let sacred cows intervene. It is not the form, but the content, and the meaning, and the fellowship with the host and fellow believers that give significance. Weighed down with traditions, you will bend your back instead of your knees to one who says, "My yoke is easy, and my burden is light" (Matthew 11:30).

9

THE MORTAL STORM

If you are acquainted with the Bible, you know that its pages frequently present nature unleashing her considerable and awesome fury: Noah awash in all that water (Genesis 7:17); Jonah, pitching and tossing and, of all things, asleep in the inner parts of a ship (Jonah 1:5). In the New Testament, there was a storm on the Sea of Galilee that caught the disciples concerned, while Jesus slept (Mark 4:38). In the Book of Acts, we find Paul in a most desperate circumstance on the mighty Mediterranean (Acts 27:41). But tornadoes, hurricanes, floods, and lightnings are not the worst. Strange as it may sound, puny man can, and often has outdone nature in her most violent behavior. The cannons of Hitler, for example, cast a more ominous shadow over Europe than all the clouds of the earth, gathered together over that historic continent, ever could have done. And then, of course, there is the Bomb.

The greatest storms, however, are neither in nature, nor on battlefields, but within the hearts of men. All of which leads me to one of my favorite Bible verses.

"Christ lives in me" (Galatians 2:20). "The son of God who loved me and gave himself for me" (Galatians 2:20). "For me to live is Christ and to die is gain" (Philippians 1:21). All these and more are Pauline words of grandeur, eloquence, and beauty. Many Christians have framed verses like these and have them hanging on the walls of their homes. But there is another text, totally different in mood and spirit, that pulls and draws my eye repeatedly. "I do not do the good I want, but the evil I do not want is what I do" (Romans 7:19, RSV). The King James Version translates as follows: "For the good that I would I do not; but the evil which I would not, that I do." Short of quoting the whole chapter, we should at least add: "I see in my members another law at war with the law of my mind and making me captive to the law of sin which dwells in my members" (Romans 7:23).

The words are hardly the kind you would frame and hang on the wall of your living room, though you might well suspend them from the wall of your heart. These are words that point to the war within, the mortal storm whose inner gales seldom, if ever, abate. If it seems strange that these are my favorite words of Paul, even above his gospel texts, it is only because the latter are made the more meaningful by the former. Paul's low view of self invested his gospel song with deeper resonance.

I remember that when I was a boy I looked upon all ministers as very holy people. It is true that they counted themselves as sinners too, and said as much from pulpits. But this, I thought, was protocol. It was a proper display of humility and generosity, filled with psychology so as not to discourage too greatly all the sinners in the pews who — let's face it — were for the most part pretty deep down in the hole. Ministers, I thought, were far more perfect than they were sinful. They lived on higher levels. Mankind was divided into men, women, and preachers. The former were just plain sinners, while the latter lived in manses, vicarages, and parsonages, not just next door to the church, but next door to heaven as well. It occurred to me, therefore, that whatever I might become, it could never be a minister. I wasn't all that good.

Now that I am a member of the cloth, I remember on occasion that there are still those who have ideas of clergymen like my own were once. "Of course, ministers are not perfect," I was told in my study by a visitor, "but they are a notch above their fellows in the faith, in holiness, and grace." When I looked as if to question this, I was told that, at any rate, ministers should be holier and more just. I quite agree. But shouldn't everyone?

Where is the idea spawned that ministers are not quite human? Some ministers, I'm sure, encourage this notion by their holier-than-thou demeanor. But, only a few. Most of them know that their ordination through "the laying on of hands" (Acts 13:3) did not suddenly transform them into bright angels of the sky. When a man rises from his knees from that solemn moment whereby he enters into the ministry of the Word, he is the same person he was five minutes before. There is no magic. There is no spiritual transformation to perfection. There is no sudden elevation from weak humanity.

Should you not believe this, I shall not blame you for not taking my word. There are better and higher representatives of my office whom you may wish to consult before making judgment. Let us together, therefore, consult the best preacher that we can find, if I may say it this way, the best man in my field. That man was Paul.

Paul's ordination took place in Antioch. Brilliant, gifted, a man of experience, he had turned from opposing to promulgating the Christian gospel. His first attempts at preaching had been none too successful. Reverses, however, developed his patience and his grace. When he finally set out on his preaching missions, traveling in an age in which it was not easy to go great distances, he suffered beatings and imprisonments. Yet always he remained undaunted and preached the Word (2 Timothy 4:2).

He was, in short, the prince of preachers. You find yourself thinking that if anybody is perfect, it is Paul. You find yourself believing that if only one man died and went to heaven, it was the man of Tarsus. You find yourself assuming that when he died, the gates of heaven were not only open, but flung wide by God Himself, for the reception of the greatest missionary, the greatest writer, the greatest preacher the church has ever had and the Holy Spirit has ever used.

But wait. Saint Paul was no saint, if I make my meaning clear. Notice how, in those words we have just cited, he allows us a peek into his heart. He confesses that the good he wants, he doesn't do; and the evil he doesn't want, he does. And so he finds a war within; a mortal storm; a conflict between the laws of his mind and the law of his members, with victory so often going to the latter, and resulting in his captivity to sin. It all issues into that groan "O wretch that I am!" (Romans 7:24).

It's hard to hear. Yet, I for one cannot be too grateful to Paul for thus admitting me to the inner sanctuary of his life, sharing with me the deepest secrets of his soul.

When Jesus was on this earth, He went into the wilderness and there was tempted by the devil. How do we know this? Somewhere, some time thereafter, Jesus told His disciples all about it and it was recorded for us to read (Matthew 4:1). How helpful that Jesus pulled back the curtain of this part of His life that we might have a glimpse. How often when we are tempted we pray and remind ourselves that we are petitioning before one who Himself was tempted and who, therefore, knows our feelings.

Paul draws back his curtain too. When Jesus

does this, we see Christ's spotless divinity. When Paul does so, we see Paul's spotted humanity. In both cases, we are comforted. In the latter instance, which is our present concern, we conclude that if Paul had great struggles too, then, perhaps there is hope for us as well, as we wrestle with such things as we feel too ashamed to name.

Paul was ordained. The elders of the church had laid their hands on him. He rose from that moment, and not just from his knees. His travels as a missionary broadened his spirituality. He lifted the church from the mire of provincialism. He proclaimed a roomy religion. Yet, all the while, he was a man, a mere man, a sinful man. There was a raging war within, a civil war; and of all the wars there are, this type is the most damaging of all.

That's the way it was in the soul of Paul. His regenerated heart was pitted against the old nature in him, dying, yet not dead. These are the greatest opposites and greatest enemies in the world. Sooner will democracy and communism come together and go together than will the law of God and the law of sin in a man, the old nature and the new. This is the titanic struggle for the Christian. It is carried on within, and continues, a three-score-and-ten-year war, until he dies. Sometimes the regenerated self wins a skirmish, but oftentimes it is the old nature that takes the victory. Thus, in Romans 7 Paul shows his bleeding heart. In the Gospels we read of the demon-possessed being "torn" (Mark 1:26). Paul was "torn" no less, and so Romans 7 needs artful and soulful reading.

But who can read it well enough? If I had the tongues of angels, I could still not do justice to those words — "Wretched man that I am! Who will deliver me from this body of death?" (Romans 7:24). These words depict Paul with a burden that he could not bear and could not cast off. Picture Paul, if you will, delighting in the law of God, yet yielding, unwillingly plunging into sin while the voice of God rang through his mind in protest. Is it any wonder that in Romans 7 Paul loses his composure and breaks forth into one of the most sorrowful elegies to be found in all the Bible?

I have heard it said that Romans 7 is a monotonous chapter. It seems filled with repetition. Beginning in verse 14, Paul describes his carnal self and his spiritual self. He then repeats this description, and at verse 25 does it yet again. Some charge that this is dull writing. Yet does not the power of this passage lie in this very monotony? Is this not Paul's way of delineating the awful trial of his soul? Paul gives himself away in these verses, and never did a man reveal his secrets more openly, or to a better purpose.

You wonder, perhaps, if you are good enough to partake of communion. It helps to hear the officiating clergyman say that the sacrament is not designed to discourage the penitent hearts of believers as if none might come to the supper but those who are without sin. Still, you hesitate because, if the truth were known, you are the greatest of ne'er-do-wells. Your face is only a facade. Actually, you are a hypocrite.

Paul was in the same boat. But he went to communion. Not because he was so good, but because he was so bad. He labeled himself the "chief of sinners." He needed the strength the sacrament could give for the storm within that he sought to quell.

*   *   *   *   *

In approaching the table of the Lord, you do well to read, and even memorize, Romans 8:1. If the stormy Sea of Galilee on which the disciples once pitched and rolled is like the tempests of Romans 7, then the first verse of the eighth chapter is like the voice of Jesus saying to the winds and waves, "Peace, be still" (Mark 4:39). The quiet reassurance of a communion hour, if participated in prayerfully and humbly, is like a calm after a storm.

10

PAST: IMPERFECT

What appears under the above heading may be the most important chapter in this book. I hope that you will stay with it to the end, even though it may become a bit involved. I shall begin with a reference to Tim and Jim who, many years ago, were the best of friends. When their church split over a doctrinal question, Tim's family joined one group, and Jim's the other. After this, they were no longer on speaking terms. Meeting each other on Sunday mornings, on what had become opposite ways to church, one or the other would cross the street to avoid embarrassing confrontations. Thus, passing distantly, each went to his own place of worship to repeat the same words: "I believe in God the Father Almighty, Maker of heaven and earth."

The end of the story was sad in that Jim became ill and died; but happy in that before he breathed his last, Tim visited him in the hospital where two brothers in the faith, who never should have allowed their relationship to be destroyed, were reconciled.

All of which brings us back to Paul. These words that he wrote to the Ephesians were not only of surpassing beauty, but among the most needed in the church: "I therefore, a prisoner of the Lord, beg you to lead a life worthy of the calling to which you have been called, with all lowliness and meekness, with patience, forbearing one another in love, eager to maintain the unity of the spirit in the bond of peace. There is one body and one spirit, just as you were called to the one hope that belongs to your call, one Lord, one faith, one baptism, one God and Father of us all, who is above all and through all and in all" (Ephesians 4:1-6).

Tim and Jim forgot about these words. But so did Paul! In our first chapter, we said that Paul always tried to practice what he preached; and this is true. It is equally accurate to observe that he did not always succeed. "Do as I say, not as I do," are words that must be spoken by all preachers, including Paul, for their lives do not always underline their words.

Paul's exhortation to the Ephesians is a case in point. He said, "We must endeavor to keep the unity of the spirit in the bond of peace." However, during and immediately after his first missionary journey, unity was almost shredded and peace destroyed. Listen to Acts 15:2: "...Paul and Barnabas had no small dissension and debate with them." Or, hear the discordant sounds of Acts 15:39: "There arose a sharp contention, so that they separated from each other."

The Book of Acts is a wonderful book. It chronicles the thrilling early days of the New Testament church with whole pages of Christian heroism, devotion to duty, and trust in God, amid overwhelming difficulties in a hostile world. Accordingly, there are those who romanticize and rhapsodize over this period in church history, whose whole Bible, when it comes to church affairs, is exclusively this particular book of the sacred canon. They constantly attempt to duplicate, in every way, those early days of the disciples and apostles. I know of a congregation that observes weekly holy communion, foot-washing, and whatever else can be drawn from the pages of the early New Testament church. In discussions with some of its members, I have discovered that, in their sight, the early church and its membership could do no wrong.

But it could. And did. We shall not ponder the details of Paul's missionary journeys except to point out that in the first of these, Christians then, as now, Paul included, had feet of clay. To begin at the beginning, it is necessary to cite Acts 13:13: "And Paul and his company set sail from Paphos, and came to Perga in Pamphylia. And John left them and returned to Jerusalem."

It is noteworthy that in this verse of Scripture, Paul is mentioned first. Before, it was always "Barnabas and Paul" (Acts 11:30). Now the order of their names is reversed. It seems, then, that Paul became the leader and the dominant figure soon after joining forces with the man who, at the beginning, was his superior.

What is more important to note is that "John," who is mentioned in this verse, was none other than "John Mark," a nephew of Barnabas whom the latter had taken along on the first missionary journey. He seems to have been the kind of enthusiast whose spirit could wane as quickly as it could rise. No doubt he reacted with energetic joy on learning that he would be permitted to accompany his uncle. No doubt the latter was equally delighted to have his young relative submitted to a broadening experience, and one that might kindle in him too a zeal for mission work.

But Mark's enthusiasm could flicker as well as blaze, which is what happened. The world, it appeared, was big and endless, with third-class travel arrangements and many nights spent in flea-bitten caravansaries. Besides discomfort, there was even more in the nature of abuse, as Paul so eloquently described in 2 Corinthians 11. On discovering this, Mark decided that he wanted none of it. He decided to return home. Barnabas viewed this development with some tolerance and understanding. He was that type. Besides, being a protective uncle, he was prone to be indulgent. Paul, however, took a dimmer view of this dropout who, though in better physical condition because of his youth, seemed soft and frightened.

As a minister I cannot pass over this incident without comment. Young people who have, or will profess their faith in Christ and follow Him, must know beforehand that living for the Master is no mere outing. It is not a Sunday School picnic where all is fun and frolic. It is well to know this and therefore to "count the cost" (Luke 14: 28) before commitment.

Paul and Barnabas went on from this point without Mark. They continued and completed their journey and, upon returning, related all their experiences. They emphasized what God had done, and how the door of faith had been opened to the Gentiles. Their presentations were met with great interest and thanksgiving, and I can imagine that the people, on hearing the reports, stood as one and sang the ancient counterpart of "Praise God from Whom All Blessings Flow."

The thankful reception of Paul and Barnabas, however, was like the quiet before the storm; for certain men, who had come down from the churches of Judea, brought with them some of those sacred cows that we discussed in chapter eight. Their message to the brethren was "Unless you are circumcised according to the custom of Moses, you cannot be saved" (Acts 15:1). These were disillusioning and discouraging words for those who, on their first missionary journey, had felt the fresh breezes of the Holy Spirit. Had they been lesser men, they might at this point have given up on the church at home. Instead, these missionaries, depleted in strength and energy and badly needing rest, summoned their remaining resources. They rose to the fighting of as big a battle on the home front as they had to fight on the road. We read that Paul and Barnabas had "no small dissension and disputation with them" (Acts 15:2), a phrase that suggests understatement. We sometimes speak of the "church militant," meaning Christ's body on earth in conflict with the hosts of Satan. In reality, it is a title more apt to remind us of those countless and interminable disputations that go on within the church, and of the great amounts of energies this takes — and wastes. Paul and Barnabas had scaled mountains in the provinces of the devil; and now they had to employ all their resources to surmount mole hills within the church. Nor were they the last to employ their time in such a way while larger duties waited.

A council was called and held in the city of Jerusalem. A decision had to be made on this matter, already determined before in Antioch and resolved, in principle, in Peter's dream. At this conference, Peter made a speech that was somewhat more consistent than his practice. Answering the Judaizers he said, "Why do you make trial of God by putting a yoke upon the necks of the disciples which neither our fathers nor we have been able to bear?" (Acts 15:10). But James, the brother of Christ, seems to have been the dominant figure at this conference. He had the last word, which was in the nature of a compromise. Though impressed by Paul's testimony (Acts 15:4), he was also mindful of the position of the Pharisees (Acts 15:5). Therefore, he proposed the following solution: "My judgment is that we should not trouble those of the Gentiles who turn to God, but should write to them to abstain from the pollutions of idols and from unchastity and from what is strangled and from blood" (Acts 15:19,20).

This verdict seems to have satisfied the Judaizers and Peter and Barnabas. It was not, however, in the spirit of St. Paul. He had a mind like a steel trap. No one could be more yielding and compromising and gracious when it came to indifferent or secondary matters (Romans 14:5). But, on principle, the man was the original immovable object, as a reading of Galatians 2:11 and the following verses bears witness. Peter, who ate with Gentiles only when Jews were not present, received Paul's rebuke, not in secret, but openly.

The Jerusalem conference, then, came off successfully, though somewhat appeasing to the Judaizers. There have been better conferences in church history. The gathering in Temple City is not exactly renowned for its "Here we stand, so help us God" spirit. But the church went on; an illustration of the fact that it endures — sometimes through us, sometimes without us, and oftentimes despite us.

Afterwards, when the conference was history, Paul and Barnabas prepared for a second missionary journey. Mark, who up to this time could turn it on and turn it off, turned it on again and wished to go along once more. Barnabas was agreeable to this request, convinced that his nephew had learned a lesson and that, being a little older and wiser, he was deserving of a second opportunity. It was an attitude characteristic of his name (Acts 4:36). Would that there were more like him. There have been many servants of God in history who did great things for Him because, having failed at first, some Barnabas accorded them a second opportunity. But Paul was opposed to giving Mark a second chance, absolutely and completely. A discussion ensued between Paul and Barnabas that quickly degenerated into an argument and, finally, bald assertions, as one said, "Yes, he goes," and the other said, "No, he stays." "Yes!" "No!" Whenever two brothers get that far along the road in a clash of wills, the end is near. Perhaps Barnabas said that Paul was too strict and rigid. Perhaps Paul countered with the charge that Barnabas was too lenient and spineless. Maybe Paul said something to illustrate this point (Galatians 2:13), and maybe Barnabas retaliated by making a reference to Paul's dominating manner in that he so soon took over the leadership on the first missionary journey. Whatever the specifics of their conversation, "there arose a sharp contention" (Acts 15:39), a quarrel as bitter as it was deplorable. As a result, these two good men came to a parting of the ways (Acts 15:39-41).

I do not enjoy relating this part of Paul's story. It represents one of the lowest points in the Book of Acts. It thoroughly reveals a past imperfect. Barnabas went one way and took Mark with him. Paul went another way accompanied by Silas. How many splits and schisms have we had since then? When Paul and Barnabas separated, they set up a chain reaction still going on, and one we could scarcely survive were it not for the fact that the Lord, who is stronger than we are, keeps the church going. Grateful as we are for this, we cannot allow the perseverance of the Holy Spirit to give us license in this regard.

We need not end this present discussion, however, on this discordant and discouraging note. There are three brief observations we should make here. First, we can see in all of this the deep honesty of the Bible. It is a realistic book. There is no glossing over imperfections. There is no "touching up," no slanted reporting, no manipulation of the facts. The Bible tells us that David was a man after God's own heart (Acts 13:22), but it does not paint him pretty just to prove that. So, too, when the Holy Spirit moved Luke to chronicle the life of the church's greatest missionary, he did not control the writer's pen in such a way as to show us only Paul's best profile. The Holy Spirit, to put it another way, plays fair and square with you. The heroes of the faith appearing on the sacred page are not princes out of children's stories. Instead, they are people like yourself. They make mistakes. They lose their tempers. They are wrong, sometimes, and grossly so. And, as the Bible tells the truth about Paul, so it also tells the truth about you and me. All of this can only make God the greater in our eyes, that He should be served by the likes of us. It may be that this chapter in the life of Paul causes you to like him less. However that may be, it will also cause you to feel your kinship with him more. How often have you refused to walk the road with some Barnabas or Mark, or Tim or Jim? We may thank God for telling us the unvarnished story of the past imperfect of the church.

A second observation is that in all the ups and downs of those early days, Paul always recognized the brethren and the church. When he went to Jerusalem for the conference, it was his third appearance there, none of which were easy. With his dynamic nature, ardent mind, and his habit of going straight to the heart of the matter, he had his differences with the Judaizers. Being a Hellenistic Jew and a Roman of Tarsus did not help in bridging the differences that did exist. As matters developed, therefore, he might easily have repudiated Jerusalem and established a Gentile church. But he didn't. In this Paul showed his grace, his consecration, and his ecclesiastical statesmanship. He always recognized the apostles and the teachers and the elders, in short, the church. This was the measure of the man.

In this connection, let me observe that there are more prima donnas in churches, sometimes, than in opera houses; more temperamental, egocentric throwers of personal weight among the clergy, sometimes, than among movie stars; demagogues who build churches or religious movements around themselves rather than the gospel; men of talent and of misdirected drive. The story of the church is not without such independents and schismatics. If ever there was a man who could have started his own church and captured the greatest following and built a spiritual empire around himself, it was Paul. But he didn't. Paul was a man of the church. He was a team player. He did not always agree with the other leaders. He was not always so enthusiastic about ecclesiastical decisions. But he just didn't come and go; join and quit. This aspect of his stature surely deserves notice in a day when so many leave the church when they are dissatisfied.

A third observation must relate itself to the difficulty that arose between Paul and Barnabas. It was, indeed, regrettable. But Paul and Barnabas healed the rift as we learn from 1 Corinthians 9:6. Though Paul had his difficulties with Mark, he also made peace with him. We must endeavor to keep the unity of the spirit in the bond of peace (Ephesians 4:3). Did he write this self-reproachfully? In Colossians 4:10 and in Philemon 24, we read about their friendship. And in 2 Timothy 4:11, sitting in jail, he wrote to Timothy and said, "Get Mark and bring him with you; for he is very useful in serving me."

Paul went to communion. But before he went, he followed his own advice, examining himself. Doing so, he discovered that his relationships with certain brethren were not pleasing to the Lord. And so he made his peace with them.

* * * * *

In coming to communion, it is necessary that you be at peace with all your family and friends.

If not, you should make such amends, and practice such forgiveness as the Lord requires. Read 1 John 4:7-21.

11

FUTURE: TENSE

In chapter twelve of Alice in Wonderland, Lewis Carroll records the following conversation:

> "Where shall I begin, please, your majesty?" he asked.
>
> "Begin at the beginning," the King said gravely; "and go on till you come to the end; then stop."

This is good advice, especially for some in my occupation who come to the sermon's end on Sunday morning but go right on. In reviewing the life of Paul, however, it is impossible to find the terminus, inasmuch as Luke does not record it. Nor is it necessary for us to make the attempt within the framework of this book.

We need not be exactingly biographical from this point forward in order to relate just where Paul went, what he said, and what he did, up to and including his imprisonment in Rome. The record in the Book of Acts is plainly there for all to read. There is a verse in Scripture, however, that encompasses all his doings and characterizes his spirit all the way from Damascus and his re-birth to Rome and his death. It is found in his first letter to the Corinthians, and it reads as follows: "I will tarry at Ephesus until Pentecost. For a great door and effectual is opened unto me, and there are many adversaries" (1 Corinthians 16:8,9). If you should ask me to capture Paul, giving the essence of what he was, and who he was, doing it with just one verse from the sacred page, I would choose these words. In this particular text, the reference to Ephesus is not important. Substitute Rome, or Athens, or any of the other cities where he preached his message, "that is, God was in Christ reconciling the world to himself" (2 Corinthians 5:19). Centuries later, the English poet Robert Browning emphasized the importance of this same thought in "A Death in the Desert":

I say, the acknowledgment of God in Christ
Accepted by thy reason, solves for thee
All questions in the earth and out of it.

The point is that Paul was always to be found where the action was, seeing opportunities first and adversaries last. A better sum-up of Paul's life is hard to find.

It was, indeed, astonishing that he was to be found in such faraway places with such strange sounding names as Paphos, or Pamphylia, or any of those other centers to which he traveled. Some of his biographers say that it is possible that he did, in fact, reach Gibraltar, which in those days was considered "the uttermost part of the earth" (Acts 1:8; Romans 15:24).

It may be that you disagree. It may be that you do not find this apostle's far-flung footsteps as astonishing at all, but rather quite natural, in that he was representing a religion that sought to touch all nations. "Christianity," you say, "seeks all men everywhere. The words of John 3:16 embrace the whole wide world." This, of course, is true. But it is equally true to say that, humanly speaking, the Christian faith began with a handicap, in that it was cradled in a place and culture that not only walled itself, but dug a moat around the wall.

The dislike between the Jews and the rest of humanity was a two-way street. The world hated the Jews. Cicero called their religion "a barbarous superstition" *(Pro Flacco* 28). Tacitus labeled them "vile" *(Histories* 5:8). Anti-Semitism flourished as much in the ancient world as it does today.

The Jews harbored the same emotions with equal intensity towards all Gentiles. It was not true, of course, as some said, that Jews used Gentiles for sacrifices (Josephus, *Against Apion,* 2,8,10), though some of the chosen race did believe that God created heathens for fuel for the fires of hell. In view of such deep antipathies, therefore, it was indeed surprising to see Paul crossing bridges where none had existed, and climbing through windows he had first to make, and which the Judaizers from one side and the

108

Gentiles from the other were always trying to brick. The fact of the matter is that, humanly speaking (but only humanly speaking), Christianity might have remained a mere Jewish heresy had it not been for Paul, who liberated it and set it free from the yoke of confining and inhibiting traditions. Paul was no ivory-tower theologian. Rather, he was a man of two worlds, the Jewish and the Gentile, in a day when there were no other such people. If Christ was the great bridge from heaven to earth, Paul was a subsidiary, reaching from where the Son of God touched down to all points everywhere. He understood more deeply than any other that Christ had broken "the middle wall of partition" (Ephesians 2:14). Therefore, more than any other, he directed Christianity outward.

It is for this reason, then, that we find him in all those faraway places, including Ephesus. There stood the great temple of Diana, one of the seven wonders of the world. Ephesus was a crossroads, full of adversaries. A committee for church extension might have counseled postponement of the place as a mission field until hostility to Christianity had subsided and conditions had become more favorable. Paul, however, was not deterred, and he remained there when he arrived. He saw doors where others believed none to exist. As for adversaries, Paul looked upon opposition in afterthought and labeled it opportunity.

Paul had the aggressiveness of those much younger than his years, a spirit so often lacking in the church today. Our postures, as Christians, are too often only defensive. Perhaps you remember Kipling's story about a village constructed in a clearing in the jungle. There the natives built their huts and planted crops. It was their paradise. But the torrential rains descended, the jungle burgeoned, and the prolific vegetation crept in reclaiming its little plot of ground. Kipling meant to make a point not about a village, but about civilization, and how the jungle is always just a step away. Christians in their churches are too often of the same mentality and spend all their time keeping the jungle out instead of conquering it behind their flag of faith. Had Paul been so defensively preoccupied, he would never have gone to Ephesus, nor remained when he arrived.

If yours is the mind of safety, you are, of course, correct in pointing out that going into the world has its dangers for the Christian. The coal separated from the fire is in danger of quickly dying out. But Paul had inner resources, supplied by word and sacrament, that kept him from being overcome. It is foolish for an army to launch an offensive without seeing to its supplies, fatal to fly the Atlantic or Pacific without an adequate amount of fuel, ridiculous to build a house without sufficient funds. So, too, it would have been madness for Paul to take on a city like Ephesus, or any other, unless he had something inside of him that was bigger and stronger than those adversaries that surrounded him. This he had: his faith and the preaching of the cross, which he described as "the power of God" (1 Corinthians 1:18). He had that vision which had stopped him in his tracks one day, which gripped him till the moment of his death. He saw great things in all his travels, yet nothing greater than that which had filled his eye and soul one day on the Damascus Road.

Having seen Jesus Christ (1 Corinthians 9:1) he was also filled with the prospect of his Lord's return (1 Thessalonians 4,5). In the days of the great depression in America, the government created jobs employing some men to build roads to nowhere. But history, according to the apostle, was no such road. Nor was it "a tale told by an idiot, full of sound and fury, signifying nothing" (*Macbeth,* Act V, Scene 5). Tennyson in his conclusion to "In Memoriam" spoke of "one far off divine event, / To which the whole creation moves." Paul, however, always considered that day imminent, inasmuch as no one knew the hour. As a man fighting against time, he avoided a relaxed approach to his calling. The future was always tense for him, for there were other places to go, other "great doors and effectual" that were open — and many adversaries. There was a world, enslaved and desperate for deliverance, though it did not know it, to be led "to the glorious liberty of the children of God" (Romans 8:21). Paul directed every effort to this (2 Timothy 4:7); and he was never deterred by what others might do to him, for "if we live, we live to the Lord," he said; then he added, "if we die, we die to the Lord" (Romans 14:8). So this man of long ago, who could have been carried, if not to the skies, then certainly to his grave, "on flowery beds of ease," chose to forgo the prestige and glory he could have enjoyed in order to give his life to Christ through service unto others.

It is no wonder, therefore, in view of Paul's contribution by God's grace, that a sizable segment of the Christian church marks January 25 as a red-letter day on the ecclesiastical calendar, commemorating one of the great turning points of history, the conversion of Paul of Tarsus to Christianity. The wonder is rather that the poets and the painters and the great dramatists of the intervening centuries have so largely neglected an occurrence that resulted in placing the Christian faith on the road to Rome and far beyond. Mendelssohn, in his dramatic first oratorio *St. Paul,* gave his great musical talent to its expression, and we are indebted to him for the grand effort and the lyrical result.

However, the best memorial to the work of Paul, and to the glory of his Lord, can come to highest expression not in stone, on canvas, or in notes of music, but rather by Christians today carrying forward in his style. It was Paul's wish that those who would take his place when his feet could no longer move, would carry the gospel onward with vigor and devotion (1 Timothy 4:15). He forecast such days as came and are, therefore urging and counselling greater zeal (2 Timothy 4:2-5). What a pity, then, that there were those who dissipated the momentum Paul engendered, and that today so many of us take the stance of comfort and of ease.

The similarities between Paul's age and ours are striking. Reading the last half of Romans 1 gives us the eerie impression that Paul is describing the twentieth century rather than the first. His was a permissive society. So is ours. He described his generation as "crooked and perverse" (Philippians 2:15). Ours, too, is all of that. In such a setting, he urged the Christians to "shine as lights," and to do so by way of "holding fast the word of life" (Philippians 2:15,16). Whether they did is not the question now. Whether we do, is.

In answer, we must admit that too many Christians today simply do not share Paul's mission and concern. If he turned the church outward, some of us do the reverse. "Me and my wife, my son John and his wife, us four, and no more," seems to be the philosophy, not only of self-centered families, but some churches and their memberships as well, as they engage almost exclusively in intramural activities and affairs.

It is true that this is certainly not the whole story. There are some of the church who are concentrating hard on the world around. Ghettos, wars, poverty, crime, and more such modern problems, consume their time and talent. For this we are most grateful. Clothing the naked, feeding the hungry, is clothing and feeding Christ (Matthew 25:40). Paul was similarly engaged. He fed (Acts 11:29,30) and healed (Acts 14:10). He addressed himself to political and civil questions (Romans 13). It is imperative that we do the same. The gospel confronts all of life. Those, however, who would save man only by saving his environment, reverse Paul's approach entirely. Environment wasn't the answer, as Paradise had proved (Romans 5:12). It was against the Judaizers, who believed in salvation by culture, that he forged in his letters to the Romans and the Galatians his message of salvation by faith (Romans 5:1; Galatians 2:16-21). That Paul reached society through touching hearts is a matter of historical record, which no one can controvert.

What he did in his times, with the blessing of the Spirit, is what we must attempt in our similar day. We, too, must "shine as lights in the midst of a crooked and perverse generation, holding forth the word of life" (Philippians 2:16). The future holds more tension than it did for any previous generation. No Christian, therefore, with his riches in Christ, may ignore his indebtedness to this morally poor and spiritually depleted age, nor can he make his payment unless he becomes an imitator of Paul (Romans 1:14,15). All do not have his talent, and all do not wield his influence. Yet, if each of us does not in this time of history give as much as in him is (Romans 1:15a) in proclaiming and practicing the love of Christ, the darkness of the middle ages will soon seem as light to the blackness of the future. Said Edmund Burke, "The way for evil to overcome good is for good men to do nothing." So, too, we can say that the way for death to settle all over the world is for Christians to drop the mantle and the message of St. Paul.

*　　*　　*　　*　　*

As a communicant, you honor the table, not only by coming to it, but also, replenished in spirit, by going out from it, dressed in Christian armor (Ephesians 6:13ff.). You must seek to bring your host, His love and invitation, into your work and walk, all the days of the week. For you, too, great doors and effectual are open, if you will look for them. For you, too, there will be many adversaries. But, as with Paul, let these occupy your last thoughts, rather than your first. And, having been reminded by the sacrament of Christ's return, let the future, which is tense for all of us, not discourage you, but rather, as seen in the perspective of His coming, challenge you to greater witnessing.

12

CROSSING THE THRESHOLD
OF THE UPPER ROOM

Which church or denomination is the best in all the world? Which one is superior to every other one?

Two little boys fell to arguing one day regarding the relative merits of their respective fathers. Each insisted that his own progenitor was taller, smarter, stronger, and richer. In their efforts to build up their own elders, they were not above making disparaging remarks regarding each other's antecedents. The first son finally summarized his whole position by boldly asserting that his dad was the best dad in the whole wide world. The other, taking violent exception to this statement, registered a similar claim, though in favor of his own beloved parent. There they stood, two little boys completely at odds with one another. Their loyalties were as commendable as their prejudices were deep and blind.

Some of our debates are just as foolish when we argue together about our respective churches and denominations. Which is the best of the lot? Which is most spiritual and effective? I say it is mine. You feel that it is yours. A loyal member of the Christian Reformed denomination, even in his broadest ecumenical mood, will still claim superiority for his own church over, say, the Lutheran communion, while the Roman Catholic, standing by, will attest that his is better than both.

The little boys who argued will grow up and discover that their respective fathers are not ten feet tall, as each had claimed. They will begin to see shortcomings in their own, and strengths in each other's ancestors. Even so, not only their loyalties but their convictions will be undiminished, as each continues to believe that he has the best father in all the world. Now, if the fathers have been truly fathers, both sons will hold legitimate positions, though both will be well advised to abandon their earlier blanket, dogmatic claims, and odious comparisons.

Allowing for the fact that all illustrations have their serious shortcomings (this one takes no note of principial differences between churches holding to the historic faith, which, in another context, I would not wish to slight), I offer the foregoing as a thought on the subject of churches and denominations. I might not fit in yours. You might find mine something less than satisfactory. But if both of our churches, with their respective strengths and weaknesses, are, nevertheless, truly churches, such questions as the ones appearing at the beginning of this chapter can only lead to such broad claims and silly assertions as are characteristic of contentious little boys on sidewalks and, therefore, ought not to be asked.

Having established the folly of the question, I nevertheless take the liberty of asking it. Which church or denomination is the best in all the world? In all of history? I will venture an answer. Let me say that it was the church of the upper room; the congregation of the twelve. Perhaps you wish to disagree with this choice, though it is hardly likely. It is more reasonable to expect that you will reserve your judgment, at least for the moment, in order to hear me out. Let me observe quickly, therefore, that it cannot be denied that the church of the twelve had the best preacher. There have been some very outstanding ones in two thousand years of church history, but surely Jesus Christ was the best. Never man spake like Him (John 7:46). The common people heard Him gladly (Mark 12:37).

Consider, further, the fact that every member of the church made up of the disciples, had received and heeded the Master's personal call (John 1). These men had responded to Christ's invitation, most of them at great personal sacrifice. They had left comforts and profitable occupations in order to become members of the Nazarene's church; a congregation, incidentally, that held services not just on certain days and at stated hours, but, in a manner of speaking, continuously — all the time. Pastor and flock were together constantly. The twelve followed their teacher wherever He went, so that for three years He led them in their prayers and their devotions and instructed them in matters pertaining to the faith.

This is not to say that the twelve were merely listeners in a passive sort of way. They were doers, as well as hearers. For they, too, went out and preached and baptized, and performed wonders and cast out devils (Mark 6:7-13). This congregation, furthermore, excelled in loyalty and in devotion. Its members remained followers of Jesus Christ in the face of many others who defected after a time. There was the group of five thousand, and there was the group of four thousand whom Jesus fed, but, in due course, they wandered off. We read in John 6:66-68 that "after this many of his disciples drew back and no longer went about with him. Jesus said to the twelve, 'Will you also go away?' Simon Peter answered him, 'Lord, to whom shall we go? You have the words of eternal life.' "

The disciples persevered in their following even when Jesus taught them doctrines that were difficult to understand, or made predictions that were hard to accept. Nor did the inconveniences of following and the occasional uncertainties of where their next meal was coming from interrupt their loyalties. So we could continue marshalling such arguments and considerations to underline the contention that, certainly, of all the churches and congregations anywhere and anytime, this one was the best of all.

But instead of continuing to ascertain what has already been more than adequately established, let us do something else. Allow me to take you to a service of what we have labeled the very best church in history. Surely, this is not a strange desire on my part. Quite often, in fact, people will say, "Come with me to see this church!" "Let me take you to hear that minister!" Furthermore, permit me to take you, not to an ordinary service of this congregation, but to a communion hour, held in an upper room.

Imagine, if you will, that this meeting place has a balcony, and that you and I are seated there in the very first row, occupying the kind of observers' benches mentioned in our opening chapter. We have come so early that none of the congregation of the twelve has yet appeared. We can determine, however, that this is to be a communion service, for we can see a table with bread and wine on it. Soon, Jesus Christ Himself will enter the far door, taking His place at the head of the table. Then the twelve will enter; the twelve who have left all to follow their Lord; the twelve who are giving their lives in full-time service; the twelve who after Pentecost are destined to go out into all the world with the gospel of redemption; the twelve, many of whom will die as martyrs for the cause.

Then it happens! Our minds are occupied with their individual thoughts when the far door opens and Jesus Christ enters in. We hardly move nor breathe, for this is the Son of God. We hear, as it were, an unseen choir of angels, singing,

"Christ, we do all adore Thee." It is a holy moment. Neither of us moves.

But the mood is broken and the spell is interrupted. For the far door opens once again, and this time two figures appear at once, both seeking to enter simultaneously. Neither one, it seems, is willing to give way to the other. The courteous thing to do, obviously, would be for each one to allow the other to go ahead; for each to hold the door open for the other. But neither one gives way. Instead, we gather that they have been, and are still, arguing. Their voices, in fact, carry to the balcony where we are seated. We hear the words, and gather that they are having a serious and heated disagreement on the question as to which of them will be the greater in the kingdom of their Lord (Luke 22:24).

Imagine! Having praised this particular congregation so lavishly, it is with a measure of embarrassment that I receive a look from you that seems to be saying:

Contention

Soon all twelve are seated and it is time for the ceremonial washing of feet. Most churches today have discarded this custom. It was a procedure usually taken care of by an attendant. But it seems that at this service there is no such person present. Apparently this portion of the service is to be omitted. Possibly one or two of the disciples are thinking about initiating this action themselves (though if so, it is certainly not those who have been disputing together as to which of them was to have the preeminence in the kingdom of heaven). Our surprise, therefore, is exceeded only by those around the table below, when we see Jesus Himself volunteering to be the least among them. He takes the towel and the basin (John 13:4), and it is to the shame of all the others present that He must assume this role.

I shift uncomfortably in my place. Again you look at me; a glance that seems to question my claim more boldly. Is this the church, your look inquires, that is supposed to be better than any other?

Contention
Pride

The service continues. We resume giving our attention to the tableau below us, as we clearly hear the voice of Jesus addressing His disciples. Looking at them, He says, with a voice that is soft and sad, "One of you shall betray me" (Matthew 26:21). As I hear these words, I begin to question the wisdom of having asked you to come and see this wonderful church. Have I brought you to the right place? Perhaps I should have invited you for a different occasion. It is certainly apparent that this congregation isn't showing up very well. I imagine that I can see the shades of disappointment in your eyes as, again, you look at me.

Contention
Pride
Betrayal

As we continue to witness this scene, we see the anxious looks now covering the faces of all the disciples in response to the Master's prophecy.

Apparently, they are not so spiritually composed and self-assured as you may have been led to believe. I had told you something of what great Christians they were. But now they all seem pained, looking around them not only, but within themselves as well. A pall seems to have descended upon them all (Matthew 26:22). In its enveloping presence, one, Judas, rises to leave (John 13:30). As he disappears beneath us, his garments rustle, and we hear the unmistakable sound of coins in his money bag.

Contention

Pride

Betrayal

The love of money

But again, Jesus speaks. He is addressing all of them as He says that they will all desert Him (Matthew 26:31). He also addresses one of them in particular, one seemingly the most expressive and dedicated, as He adds, "You will deny me three times before the night has passed" (Matthew 26:34).

Again you look at me, with eyebrows raised in question. "Is this the best church in all of history?" you seem to ask.

Contention

Pride

Betrayal

The love of money

Desertion

Denial

Is there any sin at all that cannot be found in this assembly that I have praised so warmly? We rise to leave. Having seen as much as you, I too am of the opinion that this congregation is a candidate for elimination rather than the blue ribbon. As we are about to leave the room it occurs to both of us that if anyone here has cause to leave, it is the sinless Christ. But He is staying! Then, our attentions are caught once more by that far door. Someone else is coming in. Like a latecomer to a class, he enters unobtrusively, slides into the nearest place, and lies prone on the floor.

It is Paul (1 Corinthians 15:8). We have seen contention, pride, betrayal, the love of money, desertion, and denial, all present in the upper room. But here is one who not only intensifies, but completes the list. Paul and his plume of pedigree and intellect. Paul and his ambition. Paul and his persecution of the church. Paul, the hooligan and murderer. Paul, captive so often to the inward law of sin. Paul, disputer with gentle Barnabas. Paul, harsh with the youthful Mark.

We seat ourselves again, abruptly and hastily, to witness what will now ensue. Jesus has not banned the others from His table, deserving as they are of such refusal; but certainly, He will bar this "chief of sinners" (1 Timothy 1:15). Yet no such action is forthcoming. It is rather the opposite that now takes place. As Paul's hand, too, reaches for the cup containing the sacrificial blood of Christ, we see again that it is itself stained with the blood of Stephen. Yet, the Master proffers the heavenly food and drink to him.

Many more faces now suddenly join the congregation. Besides the disciples and Paul, we see the thief on the cross, the woman taken in adultery, the lady from Samaria, the prodigal son, Nicodemus, several centurions, and uncounted publicans and sinners — to name a few.

I said something a little earlier about "the best church." But, of course, there is only one, as God is one. In the communion hour, it comes to its best expression. Thus, suddenly, we find that we are no longer merely spectators. Christ, who once looked up asking Zaccheus (who is also present) to come down (Luke 19:5), is now also looking up at us. His eyes are filled with a similar invitation; not asking us to come down so that He can come to our house and table, but rather, that we will come to His.

We accept. And as we do, we find, somehow or other, that we are no longer looking down, but up. No longer, as momentarily before, do we feel superior to those whose lives have expressed contention, pride, and all the other transgressions. For we have considered a man with sins as bad, and even worse, whose name is Paul. In that consideration, we have discovered our kinship with all who are seated about the table of the Lord. We have all broken the Master's windows. And so we would share the cup with the "chief of sinners" and all the others, in the fellowship of the forgiven.

Thus it is that we are led by angels, over the threshold of the upper room, into the holy presence. We are led by angels through doors they

125

themselves can never enter. For on those doors, in bold letters in all languages of the earth, addressed to all mortals everywhere, these words of love are posted:

For Sinners Only (Luke 5:31,32).

TEXTUAL REFERENCES

Genesis 1:3
And God said, "Let there be light"; and there was light.

7:17
The flood continued forty days upon the earth; and the waters increased, and bore up the ark, and it rose high above the earth.

32:28
Then he said, "Your name shall no more be called Jacob, but Israel, for you have striven with God and with men, and have prevailed."

Deuteronomy 9:21
Then I took the sinful thing, the calf which you had made, and burned it with fire and crushed it, grinding it very small, until it was as fine as dust; and I threw the dust of it into the brook that descended out of the mountain.

Joshua 18:21a
Now the cities of the tribe of Benjamin, according to their families were. . . .

18:28a
Zela, Ha-eleph, Jebus (that is, Jerusalem). . . .

1 Samuel 9:1,2a

There was a man of Benjamin whose name was Kish, the son of Abiel, son of Zeror, son of Becorath, son of Aphiah, a Benjaminite, a man of wealth; and he had a son whose name was Saul, a handsome young man.

1 Kings 12:21

When Rehoboam came to Jerusalem, he assembled all the house of Judah, and the tribe of Benjamin, a hundred and eighty thousand chosen warriors, to fight against the house of Israel, to restore the kingdom to Rehoboam the son of Solomon.

Ezra 1:5

Then rose up the heads of the fathers' houses of Judah and Benjamin, and the priests and the Levites, every man whose spirit God had stirred to go up to rebuild the house of the Lord which is in Jerusalem.

Esther 2:5

Now there was a Jew in Susa the capital whose name was Mordecai, the son of Jair, son of Shimei, son of Kish, a Benjaminite.

Isaiah 2:4

He shall judge between the nations, and shall decide for many peoples; and they shall beat their swords into plowshares. . . .

Jonah 1:5

Then the mariners were afraid, and each cried to his god; and they threw the wares that were in the ship into the sea, to lighten it for them.

But Jonah had gone down into the inner part of the ship, and had lain down, and was fast asleep.

Matthew 1:21
She will bear a son, and you shall call his name Jesus, for he will save his people from their sins.

4:1
Then Jesus was led up by the Spirit into the wilderness to be tempted by the devil.

15:26
And he answered, "It is not fair to take the children's bread and throw it to the dogs."

23:3
So practice and observe whatever they tell you, but not what they do; for they preach, but do not practice.

25:40
And the King will answer them, "Truly, I say to you, as you did it to one of the least of these my brethren, you did it to me."

26:21
And as they were eating, he said, "Truly, I say to you, one of you will betray me." And they were very sorrowful, and began to say to him, one after another, "Is it I, Lord?"

26:31
Then Jesus said to them, "You will all fall away because of me this night. . . ."

26:34
Jesus said to him, "Truly, I say to you, this very night, before the cock crows, you will deny me three times."

Mark 1:26
And when the unclean spirit had torn him, and cried with a loud voice, he came out of him. (KJ)

4:38
But he was in the stern, asleep on a cushion; and they woke him and said to him, "Teacher, do you not care if we perish?"

4:39
And he awoke and rebuked the wind, and said to the sea, "Peace! Be still!"

12:37
And the great throng heard him gladly.

Luke 2:21
And at the end of eight days, when he was circumcised, he was called Jesus, the name given by the angel before he was conceived in the womb.

5:31
And Jesus answered them, "Those who are well have no need of a physician, but those who are sick;

5:32
I have not come to call the righteous, but sinners to repentance."

12:20
But God said to him, "Fool! This night your soul is required of you; and the things you have prepared, whose will they be?"

12:21
"So is he who lays up treasure for himself, and is not rich toward God."

14:28

For which of you, desiring to build a tower, does not first sit down and count the cost, whether he has enough to complete it?

19:5

And when Jesus came to the place, he looked up and said to him, "Zacchaeus, make haste and come down; for I must stay at your house today."

22:19

And he took bread, and gave thanks, and brake it, and gave to them, saying, "This is my body which is given for you: this do in remembrance of me." (KJ)

22:24

A dispute also arose among them, which of them was to be regarded as the greatest.

John 1:11

He came unto his own, and his own received him not. (KJ)

1:27

"even he who comes after me, the thongs of whose sandal I am not worthy to untie."

3:16

For God so loved the world, that he gave his only begotten Son, that whosoever believeth in him should not perish, but have everlasting life. (KJ)

4:24

God is spirit, and those who worship him must worship in spirit and truth.

John 6:46

Not that any one has seen the Father except him who is from God; he has seen the Father.

7:46

The officers answered, "No man ever spoke like this man."

13:4

He riseth from supper, and laid aside his garments; and took a towel, and girded himself. (KJ)

13:30

So, after receiving the morsel, he immediately went out, and it was night.

Acts 1:8

"But you shall receive power when the Holy Spirit has come upon you; and you shall be my witnesses in Jerusalem and in all Judea and Samaria and to the end of the earth."

4:36

Thus Joseph who was surnamed Barnabas (which means, Son of encouragement), a Levite, a native of Cyprus,

4:37

sold a field which belonged to him, and brought the money, and laid it at the apostles' feet.

6:3

Wherefore, brethren, look ye out among you seven men of honest report, full of the Holy Ghost and wisdom, whom ye may appoint over this business. (KJ)

6:8

And Stephen, full of faith and power, did great wonders and miracles among the people. (KJ)

6:10

And they were not able to resist the wisdom and the spirit by which he spake. (KJ)

6:11

Then they secretly instigated men, who said, "We have heard him speak blasphemous words against Moses and God."

7:58

Then they cast him out of the city and stoned him; and the witnesses laid down their garments at the feet of a young man named Saul.

9:5

And he said, Who art thou, Lord? And the Lord said, I am Jesus whom thou persecutest: it is hard for thee to kick against the pricks. (KJ)

9:6

And he trembling and astonished said, Lord, what wilt thou have me to do? And the Lord said unto him, Arise, and go into the city, and it shall be told thee what thou must do. (KJ)

9:27

But Barnabas took him, and brought him to the apostles, and declared to them how on the road he had seen the Lord, who spoke to him, and how at Damascus he had preached boldly in the name of Jesus.

9:29

And he spake boldly in the name of the Lord

Jesus, and disputed against the Grecians: but they went about to slay him. (KJ)

Acts 9:30
Which when the brethren knew, they brought him down to Caesarea, and sent him forth to Tarsus. (KJ)

9:31
Then had the churches rest throughout all Judaea and Galilee and Samaria, and were edified; and walking in the fear of the Lord, and in the comfort of the Holy Ghost, were multiplied. (KJ)

11:21
And the hand of the Lord was with them, and a great number that believed turned to the Lord.

11:22
News of this came to the ears of the church in Jerusalem, and they sent Barnabas to Antioch.

11:26
And when he had found him, he brought him to Antioch. For a whole year they met with the church, and taught a large company of people; and in Antioch the disciples were for the first time called Christians.

11:29
And the disciples determined, every one according to his ability, to send relief to the brethren who lived in Judea;

11:30
And they did so, sending it to the elders by the hand of Barnabas and Saul.

12:25

And Barnabas and Saul returned from Jerusalem when they had fulfilled their mission, bringing with them John whose other name was Mark.

13:3

Then after fasting and praying they laid their hands on them and sent them off.

13:22

"And when he had removed him, he raised up David to be their king; of whom he testified and said, 'I have found in David the son of Jesse, a man after my heart, who will do all my will.'"

14:10

[Paul] said in a loud voice, "Stand upright on your feet." And he sprang up and walked.

15:4

When they came to Jerusalem, they were welcomed by the church and the apostles and the elders, and they declared all that God had done with them.

15:5

But some believers who belonged to the party of the Pharisees rose up, and said, "It is necessary to circumcise them, and to charge them to keep the law of Moses."

15:39

And there arose a sharp contention, so that they separated from each other; Barnabas took Mark with him and sailed away to Cyprus,

15:40

but Paul chose Silas and departed, being commended by the brethren to the grace of the Lord.

Acts 15:41

And he went through Syria and Cilicia, strengthening the churches.

23:16

Now the son of Paul's sister heard of their ambush; so he went and entered the barracks and told Paul.

23:27

"This man was seized by the Jews, and was about to be killed by them, when I came upon them with the soldiers and rescued him, having learned that he was a Roman citizen."

27:41

But striking a shoal they ran the vessel aground; the bow stuck and remained immovable, and the stern was broken up by the surf.

Romans 1:14

I am debtor both to the Greeks, and to the Barbarians; both to the wise, and to the unwise. (KJ)

1:15

So, as much as in me is, I am ready to preach the gospel to you that are at Rome also. (KJ)

5:1

Therefore, since we are justified by faith, we have peace with God through our Lord Jesus Christ.

5:12

Therefore as sin came into the world through one man, and death through sin, and so death spread to all men because all men sinned.

7:24

Wretched man that I am! Who will deliver me from this body of death?

8:1

There is therefore now no condemnation for those who are in Christ Jesus.

8:21

Because the creature itself also shall be delivered from the bondage of corruption into the glorious liberty of the children of God. (KJ)

11:33

O the depth of the riches both of the wisdom and knowledge of God! how unsearchable are his judgments, and his ways past finding out! (KJ)

13:1

Let every person be subject to the governing authorities. For there is no authority except from God, and those that exist have been instituted by God.

14:5

One man esteems one day as better than another, while another man esteems all days alike. Let every one be fully convinced in his own mind.

15:24

I hope to see you in passing as I go to Spain, and to be sped on my journey there by you, once I have enjoyed your company for a little.

1 Corinthians 1:18

For the word of the cross is folly to those who are perishing, but to us who are being saved it is the power of God.

9:1

Am I not free? Am I not an apostle? Have I not seen Jesus our Lord? Are not you my workmanship in the Lord?

1 Corinthians 9:6
Or is it only Barnabas and I who have no right to refrain from working for a living?

11:29
For he that eateth and drinketh unworthily, eateth and drinketh damnation to himself, not discerning the Lord's body. (KJ)

13:13
So faith, hope, love abide, these three; but the greatest of these is love.

15:8
Last of all, as to one untimely born. . . .

2 Corinthians 9:15
Thanks be unto God for his unspeakable gift. (KJ)

12:7
And to keep me from being too elated by the abundance of revelations, a thorn was given me in the flesh, a messenger of Satan, to harass me, to keep me from being too elated.

Galatians 1:22
And I was still not known by sight to the churches of Christ in Judea.

2:11
But when Peter was come to Antioch, I withstood him to the face, because he was to be blamed. (KJ)

2:13
And with him the rest of the Jews acted insincerely, so that even Barnabas was carried away by their insincerity.

2:16

Yet who know that a man is not justified by works of the law but through faith in Jesus Christ, even we have believed in Christ Jesus, in order to be justified by faith in Christ, and not by works of the law, because by works of the law shall no one be justified.

2:21

I do not nullify the grace of God; for if justification were through the law, then Christ died to no purpose.

4:4

But when the fullness of the time was come, God sent forth his Son, made of a woman, made under the law. (KJ)

Ephesians 1:5

Having predestinated us unto the adoption of children by Jesus Christ to himself, according to the good pleasure of his will. (KJ)

2:14

For he is our peace, who has made us both one, and has broken down the dividing wall of hostility.

6:13

Therefore take the whole armor of God, that you may be able to withstand in the evil day, and having done all, to stand.

Philippians 2:3

Do nothing from selfishness or conceit, but in humility count others better than yourselves.

Philippians 2:4
Let each of you look not only to his own interests, but also to the interests of others.

2:15
That ye may be blameless and harmless, the sons
of God, without rebuke, in the midst of a crooked
and perverse nation, among whom ye shine as
lights in the world. (KJ)

2:16
Holding forth the word of life; that I may re-
joice in the day of Christ, that I have not run in
vain, neither laboured in vain. (KJ)

Colossians 4:10
Aristarchus my fellow prisoner greets you, and
Mark the cousin of Barnabas (concerning whom
you have received instructions — if he comes to
you, receive him).

1 Thessalonians 4:16
For the Lord himself will descend from heaven
with a cry of command, with the archangel's call,
and with the sound of the trumpet of God. And
the dead in Christ will rise first.

1 Timothy 1:15
This is a faithful saying, and worthy of all ac-
ceptation, that Christ Jesus came into the world
to save sinners; of whom I am chief. (KJ)

4:15
Practice these duties, devote yourself to them, so
that all may see your progress.

2 Timothy 4:2
Preach the word, be urgent in season and out of

season, convince, rebuke, and exhort, be unfailing in patience and in teaching.

4:3

For the time is coming when people will not endure sound teaching, but having itching ears they will accumulate for themselves teachers to suit their own likings,

4:4

and will turn away from listening to the truth and wander into myths.

4:5

As for you, always be steady, endure suffering, do the work of an evangelist, fulfil your ministry.

4:7

I have fought the good fight, I have finished the race, I have kept the faith.

Philemon 23

Epaphras, my fellow prisoner in Christ Jesus, sends greetings to you,

24

and so do Mark, Aristarchus, Demas, and Luke, my fellow workers.

Hebrews 1:1

God, who at sundry times and in divers manners spake in time past unto the fathers by the prophets,

1:2

hath in these last days spoken unto us by his Son, whom he hath appointed heir of all things, by whom also he made the worlds. (KJ)

Hebrews 10:1

For since the law has but a shadow of the good things to come instead of the true form of these realities, it can never, by the same sacrifices which are continually offered year after year, make perfect those who draw near.

James 1:13

Let no one say when he is tempted, "I am tempted by God"; for God cannot be tempted with evil and he himself tempts no one.

Revelation 3:14

"And to the angel of the church in Laodicea write: 'The words of the Amen, the faithful and true witness, the beginning of God's creation.

3:15

I know your works; you are neither cold nor hot. Would that you were cold or hot!

3:16

So, because you are lukewarm, and neither cold nor hot, I will spew you out of my mouth.

3:17

For you say, I am rich, I have prospered, and need nothing; not knowing that you are wretched, pitiable, poor, blind, and naked.

3:18

Therefore I counsel you to buy from me gold refined by fire, that you may be rich, and white garments to clothe you and to keep the shame of your nakedness from being seen, and salve to anoint your eyes, that you may see.

3:19

Those whom I love, I reprove and chasten; so be zealous and repent.' "